Carol James
— Credit
— Due
— Clauma
— Referral

John Marshall

GOD KNOWS!

There Is No Need to Worry

(A guide for the chronic worrier)

John Marshall Enterprises
PO Box 878
Pine Lake, Georgia 30072
(404) 316-5525
www.graceview.us
jdm@graceview.us

ISBN 0-9740693-8-8

Printed in USA
Cover design and layout: Cathleen Kwas

DEDICATION

I AM HONORED TO EXPRESS my special gratitude to those who have inspired and filtered the contents of this book. I cannot hope to do justice here to all those who have made possible the completion of this book, but special mention must be made of two people who have resonated as a sounding board to many of the ideas contained herein.

I offer a special thanks to my two administrative assistants: Denise Olivia Sanders Baker and Catherine Davis Mills. For more than ten years, you listened to my daily rumblings, sifted through my hardly legible writings, and made really good sense of it all. You have deliberately blended professional objectivity with personal subjectivity to produce daily practical results. The synergy from our daily intellectual confrontations has propelled me throughout the writing of this book. May God forever smile favorably upon you, your families, and all your efforts.

ACKNOWLEDGMENTS

I AM THANKFUL TO MY wife, Priscilla; my daughter, Jondreia, and my sons Terrence, Marrkus, and Johnathan for their ceaseless prayers on my behalf during this period. A certain thanks go to my parents who molded the theory of "There Is No Need to Worry" into a very habit, and did not worry. Indeed my family of origination and of procreation is the wind beneath my wings. Without family, I am nothing, but with them I am who God has enabled and energized me to be.

TABLE OF CONTENTS

INTRODUCTION

WHEN I FIRST SET out to write this book, I had no idea what was in store for me. Inspiration for the subject matter of this book came from directly from life's experience—the absence of expressions of worry from my parents, but the presence of numerous expressions of worry from just about everyone else.

Don't worry; be happy! A few years ago, these were the words of a very popular song. For those who wrestle with the worry habit, these words may be just an overly simplistic solution. Simply telling someone not to do something when they have not developed the skills to stop may only compound the problem. Acute awareness of behavior may simply heighten their sensitivity, but heightened sensitivity without the tools to change may just increase their anxiety.

We know we should not worry, yet we do. We worry about our social status—even though we know we should not worry about whether we are known and duly recognized by the world. We know it matters only that God knows us. We know that is enough to encourage us to serve earnestly and faithfully—yet we worry.

We worry about what others think and what others will say—even though we know we should be like Bartimaeus, who ignored the opposition within the crowd.

> Then they came to Jericho and as He was leaving Jericho with His disciples and a large crowd, a blind beggar named Bartimaeus, the son of Timaeus, was sitting by the road.
>
> When he heard that it was Jesus the Nazarene, he began to cry out and say, "Jesus, Son of David, have mercy on me!" Many were sternly telling him to be quiet, but he kept crying out all the more, "Son of David, have mercy on me!" (Mark 10:46-48).

We know we should not worry about what others will say while they learn what they need to learn, or while we get what we need to get—yet we worry.

We worry about our marred and no-longer-perfect record—even though we never maintained a perfect record anyway. We know that no one will have a perfect record except for the blood of Jesus by the grace of God—yet we worry.

Several years ago while in the midst of lecturing on stress, I developed chest and arm pains. Thinking that these might be early symptoms of a heart condition, I promptly scheduled a medical exam. After the doctor thoroughly examined me, he suggested that my symptoms were stress related. I remarked, "Doc, this cannot be stress; I am in the midst of lecturing on stress."

He simply said, "You had better take your own advice," and then quickly left the room. Maybe the doctor had this ancient proverb in mind: "Physician, heal yourself!" (Luke 4:23). In any case, I am sure he intended that his abrupt departure would force me to make a conscious decision to conform to my own counsel. I never had any further communication with him. Instead, I was left to conduct my own examination—of my life and circumstances, and how I was reacting to them.

I do not recall any conscious worries that were plaguing me at the time, although, as always, I had several projects in process. Each one reeled from its own set of stressor issues. Though I had no conscious awareness of worrying, I intentionally began to monitor my thoughts. Whenever my mind drifted toward anxiety avenue, I redirected it toward possibility and probability plaza. Within a few days, the chest pains subsided.

From that experience, I learned that pressures may lurk in the subconscious level and create pain on the conscious level. Therefore, we must make a conscious effort to control our subconscious.

In this book, I will share words of wisdom that will help us to do that. As we ward off stress, it will alleviate worry. As I have researched the issue of stress, I discovered that when we learn our behavior is inappropriate, it always increases our anxiety about that behavior. Therefore, learning that we should not worry may very likely increase our worry. If this sounds all too familiar, stay tuned because this book will provide the remedy to reduce stress.

The worry problem *is* solvable. The fact that Jesus addressed worry signifies that He offers solutions. We are not left with human-centered philosophies. Worry is idolatry; the solution is worship of God. Worry is unbelief; the solution is faith.

According to Clive Lilwall, author of *How to Stop Your 67 Worst Worries,* one in four Americans will at some time suffer from an anxiety disorder. For the past twenty-seven years, I have been coaching people who end up doing quite the opposite of my counsel. Regardless of how I pleaded, they continued to allow stressor events to stretch them into worry. Through this book, I now try to reach the critical audience: those who just will not give up their worries.

Chapter 1

THE HEART OF WORRY

FOR YEARS, I HAVE counseled couples who were experiencing marital conflict. I discovered very quickly that some couples would return each week having made no progress in their relationship. In spite of the simple strategies that I offered for changing the conflict dynamic, they just never seemed to get it together. Therefore, I began searching for a deeper problem. It dawned on me that some couples were having difficulty because their hearts were no longer in the marriage. They could not get it together because they did not want to get it together.

In the initial session, I now make it clear to couples that if they have already decided to divorce, they need a lawyer, not a counselor. However, if they really want to work on their relationship, I would be more than happy to help. We then proceed to help them bring back their heart for marriage and for each other. The remainder of the first session arms them with communication skills that will hopefully cause them to "like" each other again. Life is a heart issue.

When the heart is right, we can see clearly. When the heart is not right, our vision is clouded. That is why my counseling sessions now focus on getting to the heart issue.

Jesus always centered His concerns and taught on the heart of the matter. He knew that the heart of the human problem was the problem of the human heart. Indeed, He knew that all human behavior flowed from the heart. Once when interrogated by His critics, Jesus picked up His parabolic scalpel, ripped open their hearts, and laid them unwrapped, exposed for all to see just what was inside. After all, He said, "For out of the heart come evil thoughts, murders, adulteries, fornications, thefts, false witness, slanders" (Matthew 15:19). Time and time again, He addressed the heart in each of His teachings. We would do well also to consider the heart of the matter.

Jesus almost seemed to be fighting a losing battle with the Jews of His day. Many of them seemed to focus exclusively on the externals. Historically, they had come to trust in the form of the law with little regard for the intended function of the law. Their ritualistic mindset prompted Jesus to declare, "But these are the things you should have done without neglecting the others" (Matthew 23:23). God's laws were never just abstract rules, but rather He designed them to lead toward a functional objective. For example, the prohibition against lying was intended to foster better relationships between neighbors: "Therefore, laying aside falsehood, speak truth each one of you with his neighbor, for we are members of one another" (Ephesians 4:25). Those who speak truth with each other would lay a greater foundation for harmony than would those who lie.

Jesus reminded His disciples that their heart resided wherever their treasure rested: "For where your treasure is, there your heart will be also" (Matthew 6:21). When their treasure rested on earth, their heart resided on earth. He taught them that their heart

When their treasure rested on earth, their heart resided on earth.

always affectionately escorted their treasure. Our heart is likewise the seat of our affections. Therefore, as believers we must focus our affection toward Kingdom objectives.

Heart prohibition on earth

First, Jesus issued a prohibition. He prohibited people from placing their hearts in temporary, unsecure, and corruptible earthly treasures. "Do not store up for yourselves treasures on earth, where moth and rust destroy, and where thieves break in and steal" (Matthew 6:19). What really was He prohibiting?

He taught them not to put their heart in earthly treasures. Let us examine what He did not teach them. He did not teach that they could never enjoy wealth. If He had been teaching that it was wrong to enjoy wealth, then the Holy Spirit-led apostle Paul contradicted Jesus. Paul wrote to the evangelist Timothy giving him instructions for teaching the entire church. Therein, he did not rebuke the wealthy for enjoying wealth, but rather he reminded believers that God had blessed the rich so that they could enjoy their riches. "Instruct those who are rich in this present world not to be conceited or to fix their hope on the uncertainty of riches, but on God, who richly supplies us with all things to enjoy" (1 Timothy 6:17). The rich were to enjoy their riches, but were not to trust in their riches.

Similarly, Jesus did not teach them that it was wrong to accumulate wealth. If He had been teaching that it was wrong to accumulate wealth, again the Holy Spirit-led apostle Paul contradicted Jesus, for he wrote to the Corinthian church teaching parents about their financial responsibility toward their children. Therein, he did not rebuke the parents for accumulating wealth, but rather he reminded parents that they should accumulate wealth for their children.

> *Similarly, Jesus did not teach them that it was wrong to accumulate wealth.*

> Here for this third time I am ready to come to you, and I will not be a burden to you; for I do not seek what is yours, but you; for children are not responsible to save up for their parents, but parents for their children (2 Corinthians 12:14).

God had historically advocated saving. By God's design, wealth should be passed on from one generation to another (see Proverbs 6:6-11; 19:14). During that time, fine purple fabric, precious metals, and money were the chief treasures of the rich and famous. Unfortunately, these items often rotted and rusted with age. Therefore, their earthly treasures proved to be only temporary.

What are the great treasures of our day? We now have preservatives, preventives, and padlocks. Yet, inflation, our enemy, breaks through and steals our assets. Even now, our earthly treasures are still only temporary.

Since our heart is the seat of our affections, Jesus seeks to align (and often realign) our affections. After being converted, we need a new paradigm for our affections. Improper alignment of our affections does much harm to us.

When our heart is in temporary earthly treasures, clear vision of eternal significance vanishes. Through our view of our treasures, our eyes become cloudy. Whenever our eyes are clouded our vision is clouded (see Matthew 13:14-15). When our eyes are clouded, our entire outlook of life becomes distorted.

> "The eye is the lamp of the body; so then if your eye is clear, your whole body will be full of light. But if your eye is bad, your whole body will be full of darkness. If then the light that is in you is darkness, how great is the darkness!" (Matthew 6:22-23).

When our heart is in temporary earthly treasures, the God of Heaven is no longer our Lord. Through our view of our treasures, the devil becomes our lord. Indeed, the devil along with all his angels are condemned. Therefore, when our heart is in temporary earthly treasures, we give ourselves a condemned lord of life. "No one can serve two masters; for either he will hate the one and love the other, or he will be devoted to one and despise the other. You cannot serve God and wealth" (Matthew 6:24). Divided allegiance corrupts our vision. God refuses to share center stage. The devil is condemned. When God is not our Lord, the devil is. Whenever we attempt to team God with another, He simply leaves us to the condemned lord that we have chosen (see Matthew 15:3-9).

Heart commandment in Heaven

Second, Jesus issued a commandment. He commanded that we invest in our eternal, secure, and incorruptible heavenly store house. "But store up for yourselves treasures in heaven, where neither moth nor rust destroys, and where thieves do not break in or steal" (Matthew 6:20). What was He really commanding? Remember, our heart is where our treasure is. When our treasure is in Heaven, our heart will also be in Heaven. Therefore, Jesus commanded the placing of our heart in heavenly treasures. There, the enemy can never rot, rust, nor rob. Inflation can never absorb. Heavenly treasures are eternal.

When our heart is in eternal heavenly treasures, clear vision becomes commonplace. Through our view of our treasures, our eyes remain clear. When our eyes are clear, our entire outlook on life becomes distinct (see Matthew 6:22). Whenever our eyes are clear, we have a clear look at life.

When our heart is in eternal heavenly treasures, the God of Heaven remains our Lord. Surely God approves of Himself, and He condones all His actions. He wants to be the acting Lord of our life. Therefore, when our heart is in eternal heavenly treasures, we give ourselves a condoned Lord of life (see Matthew 6:24). There then is no divisive duplicity in our allegiance. Unified allegiance purifies our perspective and keeps God alone on center stage.

When our treasure rests in Heaven, our heart resides in Heaven, but when our treasure rests on earth, our heart resides on earth.

In view of what Jesus said regarding the prohibition and commandment about treasures, He issued another prohibition:

"For this reason I say to you, do not be worried about your life, as to what you will eat or what you will drink; nor for your body, as to what you will put on. Is not life more than food, and the body more than clothing?" (Matthew 6:25).

When our treasure rests in Heaven, our heart resides in Heaven.

He prohibited worrying about what we will do for our body (see verse 31). He did not prohibit us from thinking, for He actually encourages us to think. He told us to "look at the birds" and "observe how the lilies grow" (verses 26 and 28). He was not prohibiting fore-thought—but He was prohibiting poor thought. He was prohibiting anxious, distracting thoughts, which amount to worrying. "The seed which fell among the thorns, these are the ones who have heard, and as they go on their way they are choked with worries and riches and pleasures of this life, and bring no fruit to maturity" (Luke 8:14).

In view of the prohibitions and the commandment, He issued another commandment. As a matter of priority, He commanded us what we should seek first: "But seek first His kingdom and His righteousness, and all these things will be added to you" (Matthew 6:33). He did not teach us to deny our needs, nor did He teach us to ignore our needs, but rather taught us to allow God to participate in satisfying our needs.

We must guard against placing our needs as the priority. Seek first the kingdom of God, which is the government of God. The kingdom of God is the sphere wherein He reigns and rules (see Romans 14:17). That concept is perfectly consistent with the prayer model that Jesus provided when He said, "Your kingdom come" (Matthew 6:10). Likely, He was praying for the reign and rule of God to come more completely into the lives of its subjects. In any case, prayer for the Kingdom preceded prayer for their needs (see Matthew 6:11).

As our world becomes more technically complex, we need stationary governing principles. Many specific contemporary issues are never mentioned within Scripture, such as cloning, DNA transport, genetic altering, stem cell research, and the like; therefore, we need a divine reference point with which to examine these issues. Within His Word, we can know where Jesus stood. Also, we can know where ultimately He wants us to stand. Therefore, we can know where to walk. We must walk where the kingdom of God is the priority.

The kingdom of God is righteousness (see Romans 14:17). Seek first the righteousness of God. Positional righteousness comes automatically at rebirth. It has to do with our salvation posture in Christ (see Romans 4:21-24; 2 Corinthians 5:21). Progressive righteousness is not automatic, but comes through our behavior. It is a work of behavior. It has to do with sanctification (see Galatians 4:19; Ephesians 4:24).

Through His Word, Jesus aligns our affections. Our affections determine our priorities. Our priorities will lead us to progress in righteousness, or they will lead us to regress in righteousness. Our progression in righteousness does not ignore the fact that we do have needs for our bodies. We can progress in righteousness while satisfying the needs for our bodies.

Our sinful human tendency is to worry about the needs of our bodies. If we are honest with ourselves, we can accurately say that most of our worries concern needs for our bodies. Therefore, aren't most of our needs about temporary earthly things? When our heart is in Heaven, most of our worries will automatically vanish.

All humans seek something. The natural human tendency is to seek earthly things first. God will give us what we need for our bodies when our priorities are appropriate. A failure to place God as a priority keeps us from experiencing the fullness of God.

Whatever and whomever on earth we put our heart into become master over us. Our temporary earthly master determines what we see. We can do only what we see to do. Therefore, our temporary earthly master determines what we do by determining what we see. Our goal should thus be to remove our hearts from earthly treasures. It should be a priority in our life to remove our hearts from *whatever* keeps us from God and the things of God. It should likewise be a priority in our life to remove our hearts from *whomever* keeps us from God and the things of God.

Whatever on earth we put our heart into becomes master over us, and it determines how we see—and how we see dictates what we do. Whomever on earth we put our heart into becomes master over us, and they determine how we see. Once again, how we see dictates what we do.

Whatever and whomever on earth we put our heart into become master over us.

Whatever and whomever in Heaven we put our heart into become master over us. Then, our heavenly Master determines what we see. Our heavenly Master determines what we do.

Therefore, we must focus our hearts on heavenly treasures. We must make it a priority to focus our hearts on the things of God, and on whatever and whomever keep us with God.

Thought Provokers

1 Why have some been led to believe that it is not spiritual to accumulate wealth and become rich?

2 What are some indicators that your affections may have become misaligned? Where is your heart focused—on earthly or heavenly things?

3 Contrast positional righteousness and progressive righteousness. How do they affect your level of worry?

Chapter 2

THE TRUTH ABOUT WORRY

CAN YOU REMEMBER YOUR first worry? What did you first worry about? What did you last worry about? Are you still worrying about it? Why? Why not?

What was the situation that you spent the most time worrying about? Why? How did you overcome that worry?

A man thought that his brother was defrauding him of his portion of the family's inheritance (see Luke 12:13-14). He requested probate assistance from Jesus. Instead of dividing the merchandise, Jesus delved into the hearts that decided the division of merchandise. Apparently, a covetous heart lurked somewhere within the halls of this injustice.

Jesus began to upbraid covetousness (see verse 15). Within the context of teaching His disciples about this sin, Jesus presented the parable of the rich farm fool, and then deviated into a discourse about worrying. He made the connection between covetousness and worry; the former often leads to the latter. Covetousness causes us to overlook the fact that God will fully supply. "Do not be afraid, little flock, for your Father has chosen gladly to give you the kingdom" (Luke 12:32). God supplies the necessities of life for His people so that they can enjoy Kingdom living.

Later on in the same discourse, Jesus again cautioned His disciples against worrying. He said to them, "Do not worry" (Luke 12:22). The original term that Jesus used literally meant, "Do not be, or rather stop being, overburdened with concern." He used the present imperative, which signifies continuous or repeated future action. When the present imperative is coupled with a negative, it prohibits an action that has already begun. In other words, Jesus commanded His disciples to stop worrying. He commanded them to terminate their worry about the necessities of life.

Jesus was not suggesting to that we ought not to be *concerned* about life. He was telling us not to *worry* about life. There is a critical difference between the two. Concern leads to constructive behavior, while worry leads to destructive behavior. Concern leads us to trust God to lead us to work constructively to alleviate the dilemma. Worry, on the other hand, does nothing but place us on paranoid hold.

It is fitting and right to be thoughtful and proactive. It is right to think about possibilities and probabilities. It is good to discuss options and have a backup plan while we put our energies into the primary plan. We must be cautious. However, when out thoughts cause us to abandon the will of God, then concern has metamorphosized into worry. The transition from concern to worry can be ever so subtle. Sometimes we need the objective perspective of a trusted friend or loved one to help us see that indeed we are worrying.

Worrying is a learned habit. Worrying is a chronic habit. Worrying is an unhealthy habit. At its best, worrying is neutral. At its worst, worrying is negative. Worrying is interest paid on tomorrow's perceived problems. When we worry, we are paying interest today on money that we probably will not borrow tomorrow. What a waste. Do we want to be like the woman who said, "Do not tell me that worrying doesn't help. Not one of the things that I have ever worried about has ever happened"? We may think that we have worried our troubles away, but instead we may have just worried our troubles into existence. Job feared (worried) his troubles into existence: "For what I fear comes upon me, and what I dread befalls me" (Job 3:25).

Worrying is contrary to the spiritual character that God prescribes for His people.

Worrying is contrary to the spiritual character that God prescribes for His people. Worrying is inconsistent with the character of those who are disciples of our Lord and Savior. Therefore, worrying must be a chronically unhealthy habit.

> And he said unto his disciples, Therefore I say unto you, Take no thought for your life, what ye shall eat; neither for the body, what ye shall put on. The life is more than meat, and the body is more than raiment. Consider the ravens: for they neither sow nor reap; which neither have storehouse nor barn; and God feedeth them: how much more are ye better than the fowls? And which of you with taking thought can add to his stature one cubit? (Luke 12:22-25 KJV).

Worrying is unnecessary.

Let us imagine that we have worried often and we have worried long. If worrying was necessary, certainly we should have observed some benefit by now. If not, we must ask ourselves, "What has our worrying produced?"

When I was eight years old, I really wanted to accelerate my upward growth. For a while, I was the shortest person in the house. My fourteen-year-old brother was taller than I was; my eleven-year-old sister was taller than I was, and to my great dismay, even my six-year-old sister was taller than I was. No one can imagine how I longed and lunged for this "shorty" status to vanish.

Everyday, and sometimes twice daily, I would back up to the wall and have my brother mark my height on the wall. The next day, I would have him check my height again. During these episodes, I thought that I was really growing taller; therefore, I wanted to document every centimeter of growth the moment that it occurred.

I had read a Charles Atlas book on body building. He advocated stretching upward, claiming that intense lunges would cause growth. Nightly, I stood and stretched toward the ceiling. Occasionally, it seemed that I was indeed growing as I stretched. Sadly, each time that my brother measured me against the wall, the mark was in the same place. This sameness created much anxiety and agony. I admit it. I really did worry about growing taller.

My worrying about growing produced nothing of value. As a matter of fact, it made me feel shorter as I shrunk back into a "shorty" self concept. Eventually, I came to my senses and stopped that nonsense. Without all that activity, I did finally begin to grow.

Now I am six feet, one inch tall. And I am certain that not one inch of my height had anything to do with all my efforts or worry. All that worrying was unnecessary. It absolutely provided nothing of value toward growth. From personal experience as a pre-teen, I could have answered Jesus' question when He asked, "And which of you with taking thought can add to his stature one cubit?" (Luke 12:25 KJV).

Think with me for a moment. If worrying provides nothing of value, at best worrying is unnecessary. The very next time we are tempted to worry and are convinced that it is time to worry, we must ask ourselves this question: "What will my worrying provide me?" If we discover that our employment is about to end, we must ask ourselves, "Will my worrying change the situation?" If we are sick and the doctor's diagnosis is dismal, we must ask ourselves, "What cure will my worrying bring?" If we are concerned about the safety of our children, we must ask ourselves, "How does worrying create a safer environment for my children?"

Our Lord gave two examples that prove that worrying is unnecessary. First, He said that animals do not worry, and gave an example from the animal kingdom that argues that worrying is unnecessary: "Consider the ravens, for they neither sow nor reap; they have no storeroom nor barn, and yet God feeds them; how much more valuable you are than the birds!" (Luke 12:24). Ravens are not the smartest birds, but even they know that worrying is unnecessary. God provides everything for their lives. They never sow a field, nor store in store rooms, yet their food is always there.

Two Birds in an Orchard

Said a raven to a sparrow, I should really like to know;
Why the anxious human beings rush around and worry so.
Said the sparrow to the raven, Friend, I think it must be;
That they have no heavenly Father, such as care for you and me.

Human beings are more valuable to God than the birds are. Certainly, if God takes care of the ravens and the fowl of the air, how much more will God take care of us, His valuable children? The thoroughness of God's care for birds who do not worry should convince us that our worrying is absolutely unnecessary. He will give us what we need.

Worrying is a sure sign that we either do not know God or we do not trust God, for Jesus has told us, "But if God so clothes the grass in the field, which is alive today and tomorrow is thrown into the furnace, how much more will He clothe you? You men of little faith!" (Luke 12:28). We may know that He exists, but we don't know what His promises are; we do not know how to access His promises, or we don't believe that He will provide what He says. We sing these words:

What a Friend we have in Jesus,
All our sins and griefs to bear!
What a privilege to carry
Everything to God in prayer!

But we probably most readily identify with the words to this verse:

O what peace we often forfeit,
O what needless pain we bear,
All because we do not carry
Everything to God in prayer![1]

The next time we are enticed to worry, we must ask ourselves, "What would God have me do? Would God want me to worry about this? Is this something that God really wants me to worry about?" If not, then we must admit that worrying is inconsistent with the commission of God. We might say, "I worry about relationships." Do ravens worry about their relationships with other ravens? Ravens just do what God designed them to do, and God takes care of the rest. If we will do what God designed us to do, He will take care of the rest. Remember, Jesus taught His disciples that if they would do what He called them to do, God would take care of the rest.

Jesus also showed us that plants do not worry, and He gave us an example from the plant kingdom to show that worrying is unnecessary.

> "Consider the lilies, how they grow: they neither toil nor spin; but I tell you, not even Solomon in all his glory clothed himself like one of these. But if God so clothes the grass in the field, which is alive today and tomorrow is thrown into the furnace, how much more will He clothe you? You men of little faith!" (Luke 12:27-28).

---

[1] "What a Friend We Have in Jesus," by Joseph Scriven and Charles C. Converse, public domain

Comparatively speaking, lilies are insignificant. Their life span is short. Their duration is temporary, yet God arranged and clothed them in His awesome splendor. Lilies never worry. God gives them all they need. Obviously, we are more important to God than the lilies of the field. Therefore, if God provides for the needs of the lilies, surely He will provide for His people. Therefore, worrying is unnecessary behavior.

Worrying is a heathenistic practice.

Worrying is out of character for the people of God, and not only is it unnecessary, but it is also unnatural. In fact, worrying contradicts the faith and trust character of Christians. In His discourse, Jesus upbraided His disciples:

> "And do not seek what you will eat and what you will drink, and do not keep worrying. For all these things the nations of the world eagerly seek; but your Father knows that you need these things. But seek His kingdom, and these things will be added to you" (Luke 12:29-31).

Worrying is a heathenistic practice.

He reminded His people that the nations of the world sought after things. "Nations of the world" referred to heathens, those who were not of God. Therefore, worrying is a heathenistic practice.

If we observed a friend praying to or worshipping a flower, what would we think? Likely, we would think that our friend was losing grip on his mental reality. We know that worshipping an object is heathenistic practice, and we know that he should know it, too. What happens, however, if this same friend tells us how much he worries, and what he worries about? What would we think and say? We must be careful, because we may pat him on the shoulders and say, "I understand. You have a lot to worry about." Or to make him feel better, we may even tell him some of the situations in our own life that cause us worry. Worry is contagious, and it is easy to join the pity party.

We would never condone worshiping a flower or tree, but while one heathenistic practice garners a rebuke, if we are not careful, the other heathenistic practice can garner our sympathy or support. Why the difference? It is because we have not firmly placed worrying in its proper category. We have yet to assign it its heathenistic label.

Worrying is a heathenistic practice. Jesus said this is what the "nations of the world" do. What precipitated this statement? Let us return to the beginning of the context. A man invited Jesus to arbitrate between his brother and himself. They had obviously been involved in a heated debate over the inheritance of the family treasures, and had not reached an agreeable solution. Who better to ask for help than Jesus? After all, they must have reasoned, He is the epitome of fairness, and Scripture was the law of the land.

Interestingly, Jesus refused to settle the dispute. Notice Jesus' initial response: "Man, who appointed Me a judge or arbitrator over you?" (Luke 12:14). That response must have shocked the heart of the inquirer—yet it got worse. Jesus turned to His disciples and sought to rupture the heart of covetousness: "Beware, and be on your guard against every form of greed" (verse 15). Imagine how the man felt. He had asked Jesus for help to receive what he would claim rightfully belonged to him, but Jesus introduced the notion of greed.

And it got even worse. Jesus then told the parable of a successful farmer. His agricultural skills had produced more than his carpenter skills had prepared for. His present barns could not hold all the harvest, and the bumper crop called for a trip to the construction company. Engaging in self-talk, the successful farmer decided to tear down his barns, build bigger barns, and enjoy life for many years to come. It sounded like a good plan in response to the abundance of wise agricultural practices—but God called him a fool. Why? The man obviously was wise enough to know what to plant, when, where, and how to nourish the fields to produced a bountiful harvest. Still God called him a fool.

The word *fool* interests me. Synonyms for fool are *buffoon, clown, idiot,* and *simpleton.* Why did God call him a fool? It was not because he was agriculturally unwise (because he wasn't), but because he was spiritually unwise. God called him a fool because the man was rich toward himself but poor toward God (see verse 21). His false sense of security relied upon his wealth. He planned his future alone, without consulting God. He was a fool because he had only earthly treasures (physical riches), but not heavenly treasures (spiritual riches). Indeed a man is a fool who talks himself into believing that he has a long lease on life. A man is a fool who talks himself into believing that he can truly enjoy life while cutting God out of his future plans.

This malady of heart is the connecting point to Jesus' discourse on worry. "And He said to His disciples, 'For this reason….'" (verse 22). What Jesus says about worry is His response to what has been stated about greed, covetousness, and poverty toward God. People of the world who are greedy, covetous, and poor toward God usually do not trust God. Therefore, they worry about providing for themselves the necessities of life rather than relying on God to bless them with those necessities. Often they live as if God has left them to fend for themselves without His aid.

Worrying is unnatural for the people of God.

Worrying is behavior for the heathens, not for the people of God. There are two reasons why worrying is unnatural for the people of God. First, God is aware of what His people need. If this is so, then worrying is unnatural for His people. Look at verse 30 again: "For all these things the nations of the world eagerly seek; but your Father knows that you need these things." No human need creeps in unbeknownst to God. No legitimate human need comes in without God's concern to satisfy it. The heavenly Father knows what we need. He knows that we need those necessities of life and He never forgets. Neither is He incapable of providing.

Imagine working some place that is a great distance from drinking water. While we continue to work, a coworker goes to obtain numerous other work items along with some drinking water. While we continue to work, we develop a burning thirst. As we wait for the coworker to return, we begin to wonder, "Will he remember all the items? Will all the items be available? Will he be able to bring all the items? And by the way, will he remember and be able to bring water, also?" The thirstier we become, the more we wonder about the water. The more we wonder about the water, the more we begin to worry about satisfying our thirst. Why are we concerned? Why are we worried about water? We worry because we have become unsure about our coworker's remembrance, willingness, and ability to bring water.

Those who worry about the necessities of life worry for the same reasons. They worry because they are unsure about God's remembrance, willingness, and ability to provide. It is natural for heathens to be unsure about God's motive and ability, but it is unnatural for the people of God to be unsure about God's motive and ability. Worrying really is out of character for the people of God, because God is aware of our needs, He is willing to meet our needs, and time and time again, He has proven His ability to meet needs.

The second reason why worrying is unnatural for the people of God is because He has assured us that He will provide for our needs. He argues from the animal kingdom: "But seek His kingdom, and these things will be added to you. Do not be afraid, little flock, for your Father has chosen gladly to give you the kingdom" (Luke 12:31-32). Indeed, God is aware of our needs and has assured us of His willingness to meet all our needs.

When we were children, did we worry about whether we were going to have water at home to drink? Of course not. We never worried about drinking water. Likely, we never gave it a second thought. We knew that our parents knew we had to have water. We believed that our parents wanted us to have water. And we believed that our parents were able to provide water. Therefore, we never worried about water.

We must apply that same rationale to our heavenly Father. We must know that our heavenly Father knows we have needs. We must believe that He wants us to have our needs satisfied. And we must believe that He is able to provide.

We must know the truth about worry—that it is unnecessary, a heathenistic practice, and unnatural for the people of God.

Thought Provokers

1 What does covetousness have to do with worrying?

2 How will you know when you have moved from concern to worry?

3 In what ways has your worry caused you to act more like a heathen than a child of God?

Chapter 3

THE COST OF WORRY

ONE OF THE REASONS that Jesus admonished His disciples to stop worrying about the provisions for life was because He knew the high cost of worrying. We really cannot afford to worry. The cost is simply too high to pay. Our response may be, "I've been worrying all my life. What do you mean I cannot afford to worry? And what do you mean that the cost is too high to pay?" In the previous chapter, we saw that worrying does nothing to help our situation. In fact, it takes from us. We must pay a very high cost for worry. Let us look at three of those costs.

> ∞
> *We really cannot afford to worry.*
> ∞

Cost #1: Distress to the mind

Worrying stresses the mind. Worrying puts unnecessary pressure on the mind. The word *worry* comes from a word that means "to disturb or distress." And that is exactly what worrying does to the mind. It distresses the mind.

Worrying forces the mind away from the solutions to the problem, and instead focuses the mind on constantly stating the problem. Chronic worriers constantly state their problems. They become very proficient at stating their problem. They learn how to rephrase and rehash their problem in seventeen different ways. Often, as others attempt to lead them away from a constant rehearsal of their problem, they simply return and restate the problem in a different way.

Professional problem staters spend little energy seeking solutions. They have no time to solve their problem, because they are constantly stating the problem. Constantly stating the problem only serves to magnify their perception of the problem. Worrying keeps forcing their mental and emotional energy to come up with new and creative ways to re-state the problem, rather than creative ways to solve the problem.

Worrying keeps forcing their mental and emotional energy to come up with new and creative ways to re-state the problem, rather than creative ways to solve the problem.

Chronic worriers enjoy telling everyone why they worry. It gives them a great feeling of accomplishment to convince others that their worrying is justified. Worriers have a low tolerance for non-worriers. They become irritated toward those who refuse to worry. In fact, worriers seem to see themselves as more compassionate than those who do not worry with them. Those who refuse to worry with them receive the label of "selfish, uncaring" ones. Worriers believe that non-worriers are unconcerned about human welfare. Worriers seek validation. When they receive validation for worrying, their mission is then accomplished. They really believe that worrying a sign of maturity.

When husbands and wives clash, one of the reasons can be that one is a worrier and one refuses to worry. The wife, for example, may worry. The husband does not or at least does not express his worries verbally and visibly. The wife says, "What's the matter with you? Aren't you concerned? That boy has not gotten home yet, and it's past 1:00 a.m. How in the world can you go to bed and sleep? Something may have happened to him!"

The husband simply raises his snoring three decibels higher and drowns out her ravings. Some hours later, the husband awakens in time to hear a cheerful, "Mom, are you still up?" as the well-past-curfew son strides into the house. The wife may honestly believe that she is more caring because she cannot sleep, but rather worries. She has even told herself that her worry has something to do with the pain she bore and the blood she shed during childbirth. Since the father did not share in the pain, so she thinks, he could not possibly be concerned enough to worry. However, this belief system is far from true.

Lest you slam this book shut because you think that I am gender-bashing, often the roles are reversed. The father may be the one who worries while the wife trusts. It is quite common for a marriage to consist of one spouse who trusts and one who worries. Who said opposites no longer attract?

A normal day in the life of Jesus brings us into the living room of two sisters who were opposites. It seems that Jesus had a knack for finding Himself in the company of siblings who were at odds with each other. Remember the brother who felt that he had been cheated out of the family inheritance (see Luke 12:13-14)?

Martha was a chronic worrier. Luke tells of an evening with Jesus in the home of these two female ministry supporters.

> ∞
> *Martha was a*
> *chronic worrier.*
>
> ∞

Now as they were traveling along, He entered a village; and a woman named Martha welcomed Him into her home. She had a sister called Mary, who was seated at the Lord's feet, listening to His word. But Martha was distracted with all her preparations; and she came up to Him and said, "Lord, do You not care that my sister has left me to do all the serving alone? Then tell her to help me" (Luke 10:38-40).

The King James translators used the word *cumbered* instead of *distracted.* The original word meant to "wrap around, draw off, arrest, and totally dominate." Therefore, Jesus informed Martha that she had allowed her serving to wrap around her mind, draw her mind off, and arrest her intellectual and emotional energy. Her worries focused her attention totally upon what she saw as the problem: Mary's inactivity. Yet it was Martha's attention that was focused in the wrong direction. Her worry forced her attention away from the permanent priorities, and poised her attention on temporary priorities.

Martha paid a price for her worrying, and we will pay the same price. Worrying will do for us what it did for Martha. Worrying causes us to spend our time and energy focusing on those things that have very little significance. What a contrast Martha's behavior was to Mary's. While Mary was sitting at the feet of Jesus, she heard His word (see verse 39). Complimenting her, Jesus remarked that she had chosen the good and permanent part (see verse 42).

Misplaced priorities had created the crisis in this home. Because of misplaced priorities, Martha became frustrated with her sister, Mary, but Jesus taught her to accentuate what was essential. Mary had accentuated the essential, for she had chosen the good part. Jesus taught them to accentuate what was eternal. Mary had accentuated the eternal, for she had chosen what would remain—the permanent part.

Martha missed it. Maybe Jesus had come to the house so often that she took Him for granted. Whatever the reason, she really missed it this time. Before we are too hard on Martha, let us do a self evaluation. What would we do for an uninterrupted evening with Jesus? How would we treat Him? Do we have time for Him? How willing are we to rearrange our schedule and priority list in order just to sit and listen to Jesus? Our evening with Jesus will not be in a literal living room sitting at His feet. Our evening with Jesus will be wherever and whenever we take the time to hear His word.

Lest we assume how we would answer the above questions, let us first take a simple test.

1 According to order of urgency, write a list of the ten most urgent things you must do.

a._____

b._____

c._____

d._____

e._____

f._____

g._____

h._____

i._____

j._____

2 For each task on your list, honestly answer the question, "Just how important is this task?"

a._____

b._____

c._____

d._____

e._____

f._____

g._____

h._____

i._____

j._____

3 If you failed to do three of the tasks on your list, what real harm will be done?

4 How much eternal value do your priorities add to this generation?

5 How much eternal value do your priorities add to the next generation?

6 At what number did you place the hearing of His word?

We can learn a lot about our priorities by taking this simple test. Too often, worrying focuses our mind on things that are temporary and insignificant. Like Martha, we can easily miss the permanent and significant issues of life—and that is a high cost to pay.

Cost #2: Distress to the body

The original term translated as *worry* can also mean "to choke and constrict." That is exactly what worrying does to the physical body. Health professionals have proven that worrying contributes to many illnesses—ulcers, diabetes, migraine headaches, and other kinds of illnesses.

When we worry, physical and chemical changes take place in our bodies. When we worry, our bodies begin to pump out an array of chemicals (such as adrenaline) that increase the flow of blood and oxygen to our brain and skeletal muscles. Our blood also clots faster, ready to repair any injuries we sustain in our "fight or flight."

I have known physicians who refocused their treatment program from treating the physical to treating the emotional. When the problem is emotional, remedies that normally cure the physical maladies seldom provide much relief. Sometimes people lose weight because of worry. Some would immediately say that is a good thing, but weight loss that is due to worrying is not good at all. It is a sign that the body is under distress.

From 1978 to 1984, I worked for the Bell Telephone Company as a service representative. The last two years of that period, I worked for Southwestern Bell, located in Jonesboro, Arkansas. During the early days with the company, I was the only man and the only Negro working in my particular office. Imagine that, working with forty Caucasian women. What an exposure to a different culture and the other gender.

This office had always been lily white and had been absent of the male species for quite a while. Therefore, the women had become accustomed to open female talk without any censure. More than once, I heard a woman speak profusely about having fallen out of love or having been disowned or betrayed by a significant other. The woman would worry herself to the point of losing her appetite; she would stop eating and lose weight. If one must enter a weight loss program, it is not good to enter one this way.

I learned a lot about worry during those days—particularly the high cost one must pay in order to worry. This, of course, did not start then, nor did it end then. Jesus predicted a series of chaotic events to come:

"But when you see Jerusalem surrounded by armies, then recognize that her desolation is near. Then those who are in Judea must flee to the mountains, and those who are in the midst of the city must leave, and those who are in the country must not enter the city; because these are days of vengeance, so that all things which are written will be fulfilled. Woe to those who are pregnant and to those who are nursing babies in those days; for there will be great distress upon the land and wrath to this people; and they will fall by the edge of the sword, and will be led captive into all the nations; and Jerusalem will be trampled under foot by the Gentiles until the times of the Gentiles are fulfilled. There will be signs in sun and moon and stars, and on the earth dismay among nations, in perplexity at the roaring of the sea and the waves, men fainting from fear and the expectation of the things which are coming upon the world; for the powers of the heavens will be shaken" (Luke 21:20-26).

These events would cause great distress upon those who witnessed them. Those who witnessed would faint from fear. The original word for *faint* means "heart failure." Fear would cause one to die from heart failure. What an impact of worry. What a high cost to pay.

Cost #3: Distress to the spirit

Worrying not only distresses the mind and the body, but it also distresses the spirit. It will minimize our participation in the wisdom of God. Because Martha was worried, she was uninterested and not participating in the wisdom of God. Jesus had an intimate conversation with Mary, but where was Martha? She was in another part of the house worrying about things that were of little significance. She missed her golden opportunity to sit and listen to the wisdom of God almighty.

Worrying will distress our mind against the study of the word of God. It will cause us to be aggravated by the study of the word of God. Worrying will also cause us to be aggravated by students of the word of God.

Listen to what Martha said: "But Martha was distracted with all her preparations; and she came up to Him and said, 'Lord, do You not care that my sister has left me to do all the serving alone?'" (Luke 10:40). She was upset with her sister. What was her sister doing? Listening to the words of Christ.

When a crisis occurs in our families, other folk might not understand why we go to Bible class instead of staying home and worrying. They cannot understand our thinking. Because they stayed home and worried while we replenished our spiritual nutrients, they became upset with us. They may even have asked, "What do you mean by leaving us to go to Bible class?" Consequently many Christians will stay at home with those who worry. Worrying caused Martha to be against the study of the Word and against others who were studying—the students of the word of God.

Worrying will minimize our participation in the work of God. Worrying keeps many believers from active participation in church work. Even when good opportunities are available, believers worry themselves right out of involvement. Worrying even distressed the spirit of the apostle Paul. "Now when I came to Troas for the gospel of Christ and when a door was opened for me in the Lord, I had no rest for my spirit, not finding Titus my brother; but taking my leave of them, I went on to Macedonia" (2 Corinthians 2:12-13). The Holy Spirit of God opened a door for evangelism and led the apostle Paul to the city of Troas, but because he worried over

Worrying will minimize our participation in the work of God.

the whereabouts of Titus, he was unable to take advantage of the opportunity. His spirit was so stressed that he left the opportunity that God had prepared for him, and instead went to Macedonia looking for Titus. When he arrived there, initially he still found no rest, but subsequently, when Titus arrived, he was comforted. "For even when we came into Macedonia our flesh had no rest, but we were afflicted on every side: conflicts without, fears within. But God, who comforts the depressed, comforted us by the coming of Titus" (2 Corinthians 7:5-6).

Because Paul worried over Titus's disappearance, he had no rest mentally, physically, or spiritually until he found out that Titus was all right. Regardless of how strong we are, regardless of what we have accomplished, worrying will interfere and sidetrack us, even if it is only temporarily. The cost of worrying is too high. We cannot afford the price that it will cost as it distresses our mind, our body, and our spirit. Worrying provides nothing of value. We cannot afford to pay a high price for something that is worthless and useless.

The next time we are tempted to worry, we should ask ourselves these questions: "What will this worrying do? After I worry for six hours, what will it provide?" After we ask ourselves those questions, we must sit down and add up the cost. First, we should calculate the mental cost. "If I worry for thirty minutes, it's probably going to distress my mind for an hour and a half. Do I really have an hour and a half to waste? If I worry, I am more apt to spend an hour and a half thinking about the problem rather than the solution. Can I really afford to think an hour and a half about the problem, and not spend any time looking for the solution? If I worry, I am more apt to focus an enormous amount of time on things that are temporary, and ignore the things that are permanent. Can I afford that?"

That line of thinking will show us that we cannot afford the cost. Next, we should calculate the physical cost that we must pay. "Can I afford another headache? Can I afford for this headache to get worse? Can I afford to aggravate my ulcer? Can I afford to aggravate my arthritis? Can I afford the time and money it is going to cost me to take time off work, go to the doctor, buy the medicine, and possibly end up in the hospital?" Again, we will probably discover that we cannot afford that.

Finally, we should calculate the spiritual cost we would have to pay in order to worry about the situation. "Can I afford the spiritual aggravation? The Lord has opened doors of opportunity for me to serve; can I really afford to worry? Will worry distract me so that I miss the opportunities He has for me? While I worry about something that I don't need to worry about, will I miss the wonderful opportunity to partner with Him in what He is doing right now?"

If we realistically add up the cost we will have to pay in order to worry, we will say, "I can't afford to worry. The cost is too high."

Thought Provokers

1 What has worrying cost your mind?

2 What has worrying cost your body?

3 What has worrying cost your spirit?

4 Was the cost worth what you received in return?

Chapter 4

THE CURE FOR WORRY

WE HAVE SEEN THAT worrying provides absolutely nothing. In fact, what worrying takes from us is higher than what it gives to us. In other words, the cost we pay is higher than what we receive in return. Therefore, it only makes sense that we should eliminate from our life whatever adds nothing to our life.

"Stop worrying." That is exactly what Jesus told His disciples in Luke 12:22. The tense of the verb suggests to us that His disciples had already begun to worry. Therefore, Jesus was saying, "Stop the practice in which you have already begun to engage."

How to stop worrying is the focus of this chapter. Let me stress right now that it is not a matter of willpower. Nor is it a matter of positive thinking. If we have led a life of worry, we cannot simply make a decision to stop worrying—and then never worry again. We do have a role to play in stopping this practice, but we cannot complete that role without God's help. If we recognize the brutal truth that we are indeed worriers, and if we sincerely want to stop that sinful practice, let us take a moment to ask God for His divine assistance as we study this chapter. We cannot make a change without His intervention and empowerment.

Step #1: Increase our faith in the kindness of our heavenly Father.

The cure for worrying involves five steps. If worry is a lack of faith in God's ability to provide for us, then the first step to stop worrying must be to increase our faith in the kindness of our heavenly Father. In reality, most people believe that God is going to punish them. They may say He is a God of love, but when everything is on the table, most people have a perception of God that usually includes a session where God ultimately punishes those who disobey. My question is this: "Do we have as much confidence that God will reward us as we do that He will punish us?" If not, why not?

If we believe strongly that God will punish us, and but do not believe as strongly that God will reward us, then our faith is deficient. There exists an opportunity for our faith. Not only do we have a right to expect God to reward our faith, according to Matthew 6:2-4, but we *must expect* Him to do so, according to James 1:5-7.

A healthy faith must execute its expectations in order for favorable circumstances to prevail. God tells us that we must believe that He rewards: "For he who comes to God must believe that He is and that He is a rewarder of those who seek Him" (Hebrews 11:6). It is a matter of faith. Jesus referred those who worried about clothes as "men of little faith" (Luke 12:28). He meant that those who are worried were fearful. Faith and fear are opposites. When faith comes in, fear goes out; when fear comes in, faith goes out.

What is the solution to the dilemma? We must increase our faith in the kindness of our heavenly Father. It is helpful to assess how kind we really believe God is. What happens when we remember the harshness of God, but fail to remember the corresponding kindness of God? We forget the kindnesses that we ought to attribute to God. It is human nature to remember harshness more readily than kindness. We may remember harshness that we experienced as a child, but have difficulty remembering kindness rendered to us at that age. We must train ourselves spiritually to recall and emphasize kindness to an even greater extent than we remember harshness.

We worry about not having enough food—but according to the word of God, we can trust in the kindness of the heavenly Father to provide their food. "Consider the ravens, for they neither sow nor reap; they have no storeroom nor barn, and yet God feeds them; how much more valuable you are than the birds!" (Luke 12:24). Jesus declared that God provides food for the birds. We are more valuable than they are, so why would we worry that He is not going to provide food for us?

Now, God doesn't throw food into the nest for the birds, but He does make food available. They must work. They must go get it—but it is God who ultimately provides for them. What farmer would feed his chickens and then starve his children? Why can't we believe and not worry? The reason is that our faith in the kindness of our heavenly Father is not where it should be. Increasing our faith helps us to stop worrying.

Observation helps us to stop worrying. No wealthy man could feed all the birds for just one day, yet God feeds them all everyday. Evaluation helps us to stop worrying. Worry is helpless behavior. It produces nothing. Worry is tomorrow's imaginary expenses being paid today.

We worry about not having enough clothes, or the right kind of clothes—but according to the word of God, we can trust in the kindness of our heavenly Father to provide our clothes. Jesus directed His disciples to examine the lilies. They flourish but do not punch the clock at the grass factory. God clothed the lilies beyond the splendor of Solomon. Surely humans are more valuable than lilies; He indeed will clothe us.

We worry about not being physically fit—but according to the word of God, we can trust in the kindness of our heavenly Father to provide our fitness needs. We run and walk and exercise and diet, all to attempt to live a day longer. We should do what we can to enhance the quality and quantity of life, but we must remember that there is no need to worry. Jesus challenged His disciples to think of how worrying would help their longevity. "And which of you by worrying can add a single hour to his life's span?" (Luke 12:25). Who can lengthen his height or his days by worrying?

If we strive to increase our faith in the kindness of our heavenly Father, we will be able to lay aside our worries. This does not mean we will not have problems, but it does mean that our problems will not cause us to worry.

I once read about a group of refugee children who had been rescued after extended periods of hunger. Most of them had nearly starved to death several times. After these children were relocated to the United States, their caretakers observed gross insomnia among the children. Normally, children have difficulty waking up, not sleeping. This, therefore, seriously alarmed their caretakers. They talked with the children and realized they had been so traumatized by their previous experience of not having enough food that they could not sleep at night; their minds were consumed by the fear of not having enough food the next day.

Someone got the bright idea of giving each child a slice of bread so that they could sleep with it. This instantly cured the children's insomnia. The question about the kindness of the father who would provide food the next day had been answered. Now that the children had bread in hand, they had no concern about provisions for the next day. Really, we are just little refugee children in a foreign land. We worry until we assure our selves of the kindness of our heavenly father.

Step #2: Increase our focus on the Kingdom of our heavenly Father.

This is the second step we must take in order to cure ourselves of worrying. We must make His Kingdom a priority in our lives. This is the prerequisite for receiving good things from God. "But seek His kingdom, and these things will be added to you" (Luke 12:31). When we seek His Kingdom, He will then add these things, and we won't have to worry about them. When does He add those things? When we seek His Kingdom. God says , "If you take care of My business, I will take care of your business. And you won't have to worry about your business."

Let us say we buy a new house. We purchase a security alarm for our new house. We pay the installation fee and the monthly monitoring fee. We have thus taken care of the company's business. When we leave home, we just set the alarm. What happens now? Because we have taken care of the company's business, now they take care of our business. After setting the alarm, we go about our affairs, not worrying about the security of our home.

God has promised that if we take care of His business, He will take care of ours.

If a most-likely-to-malfunction-at-some-time security alarm eliminates our worry, what about a never-likely-to-malfunction-God eliminating our worries? It can happen. God has promised that if we take care of His business, He will take care of ours. When we seek His Kingdom, we do not need to worry. Only those who are not seeking His Kingdom need worry. Worrying is out of order for the people of God.

The kingdom of God is the sphere where God reigns, and where He rules out worrying. To seek the Kingdom is to pursue and to follow those things that are consistent with the rule and the reign of

The kingdom of God is the sphere where God reigns, and where He rules out worrying.

God. When we seek the Kingdom, we look to do and to participate in those things that are consistent with God's rule; we put that first. When we do, not only can we expect God to provide for us, but we must expect Him to—because His Word has promised it.

Step #3: Increase our sowing into the Kingdom of our heavenly Father.

Let's revisit the context and the content of the parable of the rich man in Luke 12:16-21. For the rich man, seeking the kingdom of God would have required him to obey the law of Moses. At the time in which Jesus spoke the parable, the law of Moses was in effect. Keep in mind what the man did. He had harvested the produce from his crops. He began searching for storage space for his harvested abundance.

We must not attempt to escape culpability by placing ourselves beneath the wealth status of the rich man. The principle that he violated can be violated by anyone regardless of their economic strength. God did not charge him guilty for becoming rich, nor for considering his retirement. God did charge him with failing to give to the Lord. The law of Moses was exact: "You shall surely tithe all the produce from what you sow, which comes out of the field every year" (Deuteronomy 14:22). The rich man wasn't rich toward God because he took all he had and put it in the barn. He should have taken a tithe of what he had, and invested it in the kingdom of God. No doubt he said to himself, "The Lord understands. He knows that I have a lot of years ahead of me, and I'm going to need this. I don't want to run out. I don't want to be at the expense and mercy of my children. I have to take care of myself, so I'm planning for that. I am just exercising wisdom." God had a very blunt answer: "You are a fool! Your children are going to argue about this just like those other boys did who came to Jesus and asked for arbitration" (Luke 12:20 paraphrased).

No doubt the rich man thought, "I cannot afford to tithe (give)." He could not afford *not* to tithe. The apostle Paul wrote to the disciples in the church at Corinth, and discussed a financial contribution that had been requested earlier. "Now this I say, he who sows sparingly will also reap sparingly" (2 Corinthians 9:6). What we he talking about? He was saying that the person who gives to the church sparingly will reap sparingly. He was talking about our financial contribution to the church as a sowing-and-reaping process. "And he who sows bountifully will also reap bountifully" (verse 6). Never forget that Paul called the financial contribution "sowing." We are either sowing bountifully or we are sowing sparingly. We cannot afford not to give.

When we have increased our sowing into the Kingdom of our heavenly Father, we will readily believe that God is able, because His Word says so. "And God is able to make all grace abound to you, so that always having all sufficiency in everything, you may have an abundance for every good deed" (2 Corinthians 9:8-9). This fits perfectly with the teachings of Jesus. He taught that when we take care of God's business, He will take care of ours. He is able to make all things abound so that we have sufficiency in all things. And when we have sufficiency in all things, there is no reason to worry.

Jesus told the rich man who was seeking the kingdom of God to give generously to those who were less fortunate. He was referring to the law, which the rich young man surely knew.

> "Now when you reap the harvest of your land, you shall
> not reap to the very corners of your field, nor shall you

gather the gleanings of your harvest. Nor shall you glean your vineyard, nor shall you gather the fallen fruit of your vineyard; you shall leave them for the needy and for the stranger. I am the Lord your God" (Leviticus 19:9-10).

Why would God tell His people to do that? A turnip-green farmer was not allowed to harvest all his turnip greens. He was to leave the corners for strangers and the needy. This was God's welfare system. This was God's AFDC and WIC voucher program. It consisted of His people leaving food stuff for the stranger and the needy. This approach would cure the major problem with our current welfare system. Under God's system, the needy had to exert some physical energy to go and retrieve their own food from the field.

God required the corners of the field to be left for the stranger and the needy. Anyone could look at a man's field and tell how generous he was, but what did the rich man do? He took all that he had in the field and put it into the barn. He wasn't supposed to do that. Fruit that fell off the tree had to be left on the ground for the strangers, orphans, and widows.

When we increase our sowing in the Kingdom of the heavenly Father, we will be able to partake of all the promises and benefits reserved for His people, and we will once and for all be able to lay aside all our worries.

Remember: When we worry, we are paying interest today on problems that may never surface. When we choose not to worry, it does not mean we are unconcerned; it means that our concerns never cause us to deviate from God's standard. So no matter how much concern we have about what is going on around us, we stay with God's standard. We sow into His Kingdom, and He will take care of us. God has promised that He would do so, and He has demonstrated that He will honor His promises.

Step #4: Increase the time we spend observing how the promise of God grows toward fruition.

Rather than taking precious time to worry, we can cure worrying by spending that time examining the lives of historical and contemporary people who have chosen to put their faith in the promises of God—and reaped the benefits. This will be of great encouragement to our own hearts. Worrying often grows into a feeling of haplessness, helplessness, and hopelessness. Observing the promises of God come to fruition will help to destroy those feelings.

Observe the promises of God grow toward fruition and fulfillment in the lives of characters of the Old Testament (see Romans 15:4) and New Testament (see Acts 23:10-12, 27:21-25, 44). Read about the saints of God. Study their lives. Observe the promises of God grow toward fruition and fulfillment in the lives of contemporary persons (see Philippians 1:12-14). Read testimonies and biographies, and be encouraged by their lives. Observe these fulfilled promise come true in the lives of our parents, and other believers with whom we regularly interact. And we can observe how the promises of God have grown toward fruition in our own life. Answering these questions may help: "What was the last really good thing that God did for me? Why am I so hesitant to announce the graciousness of God (and so quick to tell how the devil has mistreated me)?"

Step #5: Decrease the time we spend in conduct and conversations that fuel and fan the flames of worry.

Develop a conduct that resists worrying. Stop participating in worry conversation. Words produce worry, and worry produces words that produce more worries. Refuse to become entangled in that vicious cycle. Stop listening to worry words. Stop speaking worry words. Instead, start participating in faith-strengthening conversation. Start listening to words that reduce worrying. Start speaking words that reduce worrying. State solutions rather than problems.

We may need to rephrase our terminology. Instead of saying, "I will not have enough money for rent," we can say, "I will disconnect cable so that I will have enough money for rent." Change "I do not know what I will do" to "I must discover what to do." Counteract every temptation to worry with words of faith.

We may also need to evaluate some of our friendships. Do we surround ourselves with people who fuel worry, or people who fuel faith? We may need to decrease the time we spend with people at pity parties, and instead increase the time we spend with people whose faith we admire.

In his letter to the Philippians, the apostle Paul echoed the same theme that Jesus did in Matthew 6:25. When Paul said, "Be anxious for nothing" (Philippians 4:6), he used the same term that Jesus did. Paul, like Jesus, encouraged people to exercise caution in their process of life.

Rather than worry, we should pray. The renewed mind must break the habit of perpetual worry that long ago started in the unregenerated mind. When we worry, we do not trust God; therefore, we sin. The sin of worry stems from a heart that fails to trust God. A non-trusting heart will prevent our prayers from being answered, for God answers prayers offered in faith (see James 1:5-7). When we replace worrying with praying, the presence of God keeps joy in and worry out.

While doctors recommend prescription drugs for serious cases of excessive worry, in many cases there is a much simpler way to reduce worry—with no side effects. There *is* a cure for worry. It will not come easy, however, because it involves changing past patterns and breaking habits. If we are prone to worry, we may have developed life-long behaviors and routines that we need to stop. It is time for a paradigm shift in our life. To stop worrying, we must internalize, implement, and activate the principles that we have learned in this chapter. Often we attend seminars and hear inspirational speakers. They say, "Do thus and so," and we leave saying, "This won't work." We go home and don't do it. And we are right; it doesn't work. Medicine that remains in the medicine cabinet cures no illnesses. Medicine will not work unless it is applied to the illness. Let us make a commitment to follow the cure to stop worrying.

Thought Provokers

1 What is your honest view of the kindness of God toward His people? Toward you? Do you need to reevaluate that view?

2 Where have you been stingy in sowing into the Kingdom? Where can you sow more? What benefits can you expect? Why?

3 What are some of the friendships and relationships that you may need to reconsider as you seek the cure for worrying? What person or persons do you know who could provide a positive replacement? When will you make the effort to seek out him or her?

Chapter 5

HOW TO BE A FIRST-CLASS WORRIER

WE HAVE LEARNED THAT worrying contradicts Christian character, and that worrying is unnecessary and unnatural. We have seen that worrying is expensive; it is probably the most expensive habit in which we could ever engage. It is expensive because it distresses the mind; it distresses the body, and it also distresses the spirit. We have also learned that there *is* a cure to worrying, and we studied five steps we can take in cooperation with the Holy Spirit in order to be free from worry once and for all.

In spite of what we have learned, I know that at least one person who reads this book is going to continue to worry. If you are that one person, I dedicate this chapter to you. Since you are going to worry, you should learn how to worry first-class. If you must worry, please learn how to worry efficiently and effectively.

If you must worry, please learn how to worry efficiently and effectively.

One, decide when you are going to worry. After all, the wise man said, "There is an appointed time for everything" (Ecclesiastes 3:1). Jesus continually emphasized His timing, and He refused to be troubled before the time. "And he said, Go into the city to such a man, and say unto him, The Master saith, My time is at hand; I will keep the passover at thy house with my disciples" (Matthew 26:18 KJV). Only during the last few hours of His earthly life did Jesus agonize over His death.

> Then cometh Jesus with them unto a place called Gethsemane, and saith unto the disciples, Sit ye here, while I go and pray yonder. And he took with him Peter and the two sons of Zebedee, and began to be sorrowful and very heavy. Then saith he unto them, My soul is exceeding sorrowful, even unto death: tarry ye here, and watch with me (Matthew 26:36-38 KJV).

If you are going to be a first-class worrier, you need to decide the day of the week and the hour of the day that you are going to worry. Only worry one day per week. For example, you may decide to worry each Sunday morning at 7:45 a.m. If that is your time, refuse to worry at any time other than the decided upon time to worry. Delay all your worrying until the time that you have chosen. Refuse to worry before your scheduled worry time—but do always keep your worry appointment. Never allow anyone or anything to infringe upon your worry time.

Give that worry time a glamorous name. You can then talk to others in a spectacular way about your worry day. Some other person may need to follow suit, and you will be a great help to him or her. You may eventually be able to lead seminars and conferences on the subject.

Two, decide how long you are going to worry. Jesus prayed three times then stopped. He refused to linger longer in agony.

> And he left them, and went away again, and prayed the third time, saying the same words. Then cometh he to his disciples, and saith unto them, Sleep on now, and take your rest: behold, the hour is at hand, and the Son of man is betrayed into the hands of sinners. Rise, let us be going: behold, he is at hand that doth betray me (Matthew 26:44-46 KJV).

I suggest either nineteen or twenty-three minutes per worry session. Television has programmed the human mind to think in twenty-minute blocks of time. These two numbers are the closest two primary numbers to twenty.

Set the alarm clock so that you can worry for the exact period of time. Refuse to worry beyond the allotted time. In case there are pressing worry issues, however, and you must go beyond the allocated time, give yourself credit—at least time-and-a-half for each overtime minute. Deduct that from the time of your next worry session. Keep an accurate written record of the length of each of your worry sessions.

Three, decide where you are going to worry. Only in the Garden of Gethsemane did Jesus pray in agony about His death. "Then cometh

Jesus with them unto a place called Gethsemane, and saith unto the disciples, Sit ye here, while I go and pray yonder" (Matthew 26:36 KJV).

Select a cool and comfortable place to worry. Make sure it is conducive to worrying. Refuse to worry at any other place.

Make sure there are no Bibles within sight. Bibles or related Scripture paraphernalia may remind you how the word of God teaches us not to worry. Obviously you will not be able to worry at the church building. Reminders such as this may cause ever so slight guilt as you attempt to worry, and you do not want to be distracted. Remembering that you should not worry may actually interfere with your ability to worry during the particular session. You certainly do not want that to happen.

Do not worry in the kitchen or the dining room. Worrying there may interfere with the digestion of your food. Do not worry in the living room or the den. Worrying there may interfere with relaxation. Do not worry in the bathroom. Worrying there may interfere with elimination. Do not worry in the bedroom. Worrying there may cause restlessness when trying to sleep. You may need to build or rent a special place that is most conducive for worry.

Four, decide precisely what you are going to worry about. Jesus focused only on the passing of the cup.

> And he went a little farther, and fell on his face, and prayed, saying, O my Father, if it be possible, let this cup pass from me: nevertheless not as I will, but as thou wilt. And he cometh unto the disciples, and findeth them asleep, and saith unto Peter, What, could ye not watch with me one hour? Watch and pray, that ye enter

not into temptation: the spirit indeed is willing, but the flesh is weak. He went away again the second time, and prayed, saying, O my Father, if this cup may not pass away from me, except I drink it, thy will be done (Matthew 26:39-42 KJV).

Don't spend your time worrying about what to worry about. Plan ahead. Write a specific statement about what you are going to worry about. You can then get right into worrying at the beginning seconds of your session. There is no reason to waste time just because you are disorganized.

Be very precise and be very specific about what you are going to worry about. Worry about only one issue per worry session. If you have decided that you are going to worry about your grandson, then don't spend time in that session worrying about your children. Worry about only one issue per worry session.

Five, decide who you are going to invite to your worry session. For His time of bereavement, Jesus took Peter, James, and John. "And he took with him Peter and the two sons of Zebedee, and began to be sorrowful and very heavy" (Matthew 26:37 KJV).

Never worry alone. Invite at least three people to each of your worry sessions. Do not invite people who are worrying themselves, or worse yet, who are worrying about themselves. You want to invite people who will focus on you and your problems, not on themselves. Decide who you are going to invite, and let them know ahead of time exactly what you are worrying about, where you will be worrying, and how long you are going to worry.

Six, when the worry session ends, ceremonially burn the paper on which you have written your worries. As that smoke rises, visualize your worries rising up to the throne of God.

> And He came and took the book out of the right hand of Him who sat on the throne. When He had taken the book, the four living creatures and the twenty-four elders fell down before the Lamb, each one holding a harp and golden bowls full of incense, which are the prayers of the saints (Revelation 5:7-8).

Visualize your worries rising to God, thus obligating Him to respond favorably. This will be a visual demonstration of the concept that the apostle Peter taught. "Therefore humble yourselves under the mighty hand of God, that He may exalt you at the proper time, casting all your anxiety on Him, because He cares for you" (1 Peter 5:6-7). Trouble God, not yourself, with your worries. Imagine a burning container that is full of incense. What happens when incense is burned? It rises. Incense represents the prayers or concerns of the saints rising toward the throne of God.

> When the Lamb broke the seventh seal, there was silence in heaven for about half an hour. And I saw the seven angels who stand before God, and seven trumpets were given to them. Another angel came and stood at the altar, holding a golden censer; and much incense was given to him, so that he might add it to the prayers of all the saints on the golden altar which was

before the throne. And the smoke of the incense, with the prayers of the saints, went up before God out of the angel's hand (Revelation 8:1-4).

God requested that worshipers burn incense while they were offering their prayers to Him. This served as a visual demonstration of what they were doing.

As I describe how to be a first-class worrier, I am obviously being somewhat sarcastic in delineating the first five steps above. I am, however, quite serious when I describe the sixth step. Even if you do not actually write your worries on a piece of paper and ceremonially burn them, at least offer them all as incense to the Lord, "casting all your anxiety on Him, because He cares for you" (1 Peter 5:7). If you are able to trust the Lord with your worries, you will reduce your worries to concerns. Remember, when you are worried, the worries control you. When you are concerned, you recognize that God is in control of the situation that worries you. Certainly there are issues about which you ought to be concerned. Certainly there are troublesome issues, but as long as you are managing them, you are controlling them. You are concerned, not worried. And that is first class.

Thought Provokers

1 Which of these steps do you recognize in your own life?

2 Where have you devoted too much time to becoming a first-class worrier?

3 When will you stop?

Chapter 6

KICK THE WORRY HABIT

THIS CHAPTER COULD ALSO be entitled, "Win the Little Battles That Come Before the Big Battle." Remember the giant Goliath? Remember how he taunted the army of Israel for some forty consecutive days?

> The Philistines stood on the mountain on one side while Israel stood on the mountain on the other side, with the valley between them. Then a champion came out from the armies of the Philistines named Goliath, from Gath, whose height was six cubits and a span (1 Samuel 17:3-4).

The Philistine army was proud of their nine-foot nine-inch champion, the giant Goliath. Twice daily for forty days, he taunted the army of the living God, challenging them to send out a representative to battle against him (see verses 8-9). Goliath proposed that the victor would gain a victory for his entire army, and the loser would lose for his entire army. The army of the loser would become servants for the army of the winner.

Every morning the army of Israel got up and said, "Let's go fight this guy." They put on their army uniforms and their helmets, took up their weapons, and went out and shouted the war cry. Eighty times during these forty days, they put on their battle clothes and sounded their war cries—and then ran in the opposite direction when Goliath showed up (see verse 16).

Then there was David, the little shepherd boy.

> So David arose early in the morning and left the flock with a keeper and took the supplies and went as Jesse had commanded him. And he came to the circle of the camp while the army was going out in battle array shouting the war cry. Israel and the Philistines drew up in battle array, army against army. Then David left his baggage in the care of the baggage keeper, and ran to the battle line and entered in order to greet his brothers. As he was talking with them, behold, the champion, the Philistine from Gath named Goliath, was coming up from the army of the Philistines, and he spoke these same words; and David heard them. When all the men of Israel saw the man, they fled from him and were greatly afraid. The men of Israel said, "Have you seen this man who is coming up? Surely he is coming up to defy Israel. And it will be that the king will enrich the man who kills him with great riches and will give him

his daughter and make his father's house free in Israel." Then David spoke to the men who were standing by him, saying, "What will be done for the man who kills this Philistine and takes away the reproach from Israel? For who is this uncircumcised Philistine, that he should taunt the armies of the living God?" (1 Samuel 17:20-26).

David, the shepherd boy, did not have battle clothing. He was just the musician son of Jesse. And on this particular day, he was assigned the none-too-exciting task of taking cheese and other provisions to his brothers who were in the army. While on this food assignment, he observed what was taking place. He inquired and decided to do battle with Goliath. Ultimately, David took a sling with rocks and slung it, striking Goliath in the forehead, and killing him.

Now the roles were reversed. It was the Philistines who ran. When they saw what this young boy did—attack and kill their mascot—they were the ones who were fearful and afraid because their leader, their hero, had been destroyed. That turn of events gave great courage to the army of Israel. Whereas before they ran from the Philistines, now they ran after them. Their new-found courage carried them to victory.

There is much we can learn from this account. We, too, face giants in our lives—those obstacles over which we often tearfully and fearfully agonize and worry. Sometimes in our fear, we run from them, but eventually we must meet them on the battlefield.

Imagine that while picking up a piece of lumber, a splinter accidentally works its way into our hand. If we leave it there, every time we touch something it will hurt. Therefore, the best thing to do is remove it. Although it may be painful to remove it, it is more painful to leave it there. In the long run, the best thing to do is take it out.

Likewise, I suggest that we ought to do battle with the giants that cause us worry. It may be painful to remove them from our lives, but it will be more painful to leave them there. In the long run, the best thing to do is take them out. When our positive courage outweighs our negative fears, we are ready to do battle with the giants. People who do battle have learned to manage their fears. They still have some fear, but their courage has risen above the level of their fear. They are motivated to go out and do battle with the giants that keep confronting them.

David was the son of Jesse, who was the grandson of Ruth. David came to the battlefield in order to bring food sustenance for his brothers. He saw how the army of Israel was afraid of Goliath. He asked the question, "Who is the uncircumcised Philistine that he should taunt the armies of the living God?" (verse 26). When David developed a passion for God to get His glory and developed a pleasure for himself to get his gifts, he did battle. When he perceived that God worked through human individuals to bring about victory, David said, "I will do battle with Goliath." He made this decision in spite of the opposition standing in his way.

We, too, must make the same decision—in spite of the opposition. We must do battle with the giants standing in our way, because the giants are not going to go away on their own. As we do, we must remember that sometimes winning the war may be easier than getting to the battle. We all have faced circumstances and battles over which we agonized. There may have been a situation where we needed to talk with someone, and we agonized over having to do that. When we finally talked with the person, however, we found that it wasn't that difficult. We realized that our imagination had magnified the problem. Worry will do that; it will spark imagination. Many fearful possibilities do not exist outside of a worry environment. Fearful imagination produces worry, which produces more fearful imaginations, which produces more worry. Too often, worry twirls us in a never-ending spiral. Eventually, if we do not deal with it, it will choke the life out of us.

Yes, sometimes getting to the battle is more difficult than winning the war. David encountered more opposition getting to the battlefield than he did actually winning the war. When he finally got to the battlefield, the war was very easy. The question is, why is it so difficult to get to the battle? Why is it sometimes easier to win the war than to get to the battle? Sometimes unexpected "little" battles precede the expected big battle. These little battles can prove to be quite formidable obstacles.

There are three types of obstacles that can stand in our way.

Emotional obstacles

First, there are emotional obstacles. They not only hinder the battle, but they hinder us from even getting to the battle. Sometimes these obstacles come from within the very bonds that tie us together—as David discovered on his way to the battlefield. David observed. Then he spoke to the men. Eliab, his oldest brother, heard the conversation and became an obstacle to David getting to the battle with Goliath. When David asked what would be done for the man who destroys

Goliath, Eliab angrily criticized his brother David; in other words, he went emotionally ballistic (see 1 Samuel 17:28).

Even within a family perspective, even among siblings, there can be a tremendous amount of emotional criticism. Sometimes the youngest sibling has lived all his or her life under the shadow (emotional obstacle) of an older sibling. The older sibling can sometimes be so overpowering emotionally that he or she discourages the younger, even when not intending to.

My sister was always academically astute. I never told her so, but I admired her scholastic ability. Even though I always had the ability to maintain an A grade average (I believe most children do), I still looked up to her smarts. My sister was three years ahead of me, and during her senior year at the University of Tennessee at Martin (where she maintained almost a 4.0 average), I was in my senior year in high school and applying to universities. Memphis State University (now the University of Memphis) offered me an opportunity to enter their engineering program. Although I had not seriously considered the Memphis State offer, I still remember my sister saying she had heard that Memphis State was prejudiced, and I probably would not make A's there. This gave me more than enough fodder to remove any inkling of enrolling there. My sister never intended to discourage me by her words, but I allowed that to happen. We have never ever again talked about that remark. As a matter of fact, she will first learn about it from reading this book.

Let no one think for even a moment that my sister was a discourager. She was quite the opposite. Even now she is often the "straw that stirs the whole family shake." Being three grades ahead of me, she always checked my school work and insisted that I do my very best. During our growing up years, she took the time to teach me her school work. As a matter of fact, thanks to her, I went through most of my classes already thoroughly knowledgeable of the course material long before the teacher presented it. When I was in the sixth grade, my sister taught me Gregg shorthand. Imagine that; an "all-male" country farm boy knowing shorthand. That same year, Daddy bought an Underwood manual typewriter. I began to "one" finger around on it, but my sister insisted that I learn the proper way to type on a keyboard. Once again, she shared her materials from her typing class, and I learned how to touch type. Imagine that; I became a proficient typist while still in elementary school.

My sister's investment and involvement in my life have proven to be priceless. I cannot begin to list all the benefits that have come upon me just because of that. So how did I allow one seemingly insignificant comment to impact me so strongly? Maybe it is as Dr. Phil McGraw declares that our encounters with people and experiences really do define us. He also says that the further back into our childhood we recall memories, the more defining they are likely to be to us.

It is very likely, then, that fearful imagination about Memphis State University produced worry, which produced more fearful imagination about Memphis State University. I do not know whether God wanted me to take advantage of the opportunity to attend Memphis State University. It seems that He had other plans for me. There are no regrets about not being an engineer, and I thoroughly enjoy being a "relationship consultant." If I were independently wealthy, I would pay people to let me help them. The point is that I allowed fearful imagination to magnify an imagined problem, which in turn had the power to influence my decisions.

Younger siblings often look up to the older ones, and believe what their older brothers and sisters tell them—without questioning it. And in some cases this can be emotionally overpowering, as in the case with David and Eliab. Eliab questioned his youngest brother's integrity. "Now Eliab his oldest brother heard when he spoke to the men; and Eliab's anger burned against David and he said, 'Why have you come down?'" (1 Samuel 17:28). Calling one's integrity into question is a fine way to zap all emotional energy.

Eliab seemed to be saying, "Look, little brother, the army is already here and it is *our* job to fight against Goliath, so why are *you* here?" Notice what else Eliab said: "And with whom have you left those few sheep in the wilderness?" Now, those words no doubt really cut David to the bone. Eliab did not leave it there, however, but added more: "I know your insolence and the wickedness of your heart" (verse 28). That's pretty cutting—an attack on the motivation of David's heart. Eliab in essence said, "I know you, and you are up to no good. You have corrupt intentions."

David skillfully shunned the full force of his brother's charge. Notice something else in verse 29: "But David said, 'What have I done now?'" The simple word *now* tells us much about David and Eliab's previous interactions. Eliab had criticized David before. Likely, Eliab always criticized David. David said, "What have I done *now?* I just asked a question."

Eliab not only questioned David's integrity, but he also questioned David intensely. There was undoubtedly a history of the older brother always questioning, ridiculing, and belittling his younger brother. We can see how this response to a younger sibling would naturally zap all enthusiasm—but it failed to work on this occasion. David barged straight ahead toward God's plan. When we are walking within the will of God, we must march forward in spite of the intensity of critique. Unfortunately, others may cut us to pieces even before we finish what we are trying to say. Their emotional posture positions them in first-strike mode.

David simply asked a question. Why would Eliab be so upset by this question? Eliab was upset at David, not just his question. Was Eliab going to battle with Goliath? No. He was running with the rest of the army. Why was Eliab so critical? Could Eliab have been upset with God, and he took it out on David? Could Eliab have been angry because God had passed over him in favor of David being the next king? The answer lies in 1 Samuel 16:6-13.

Sibling rivalry and jealousy can be intense. Cain was angry when God rejected his sacrifice, yet he exacted his anger not on God but on his brother, Abel (see Genesis 4:1-8). Joseph's brothers became angry with him when they observed the favor of God upon his life (see Genesis chapter 37). Therefore, it is in keeping with what we know about human behavior that a sibling could harshly attack another sibling simply because the favor of God rests upon him or her.

This is a word of caution not just for siblings, but for parents and their children. We must keep our spiritual senses open for what God may be doing in the lives of the younger ones in our midst. We must be aware when it becomes time to release them to their own choices, however fledging they may be. Always be on guard. We never know when nor how much we may encourage or could have encouraged.

When emotional obstacles lodge themselves in our way, what do we do about them? How do we overcome emotional obstacles? We all will face some emotional obstacles. Somebody, somewhere, will roll them into place. Often it is an older sibling or a parent. On other occasions, in-laws may feel that they are emotionally over us. One spouse may feel emotionally over the other.

How do we overcome those emotional obstacles? Let us see how David overcame. "But David said, 'What have I done now? Was it not just a question?'" (1 Samuel 17:29). The next verse is the key. "Then he turned away from him to another and said the same thing; and the people answered the same thing as before" (verse 30). When his brother Eliab attacked him emotionally, David just ignored him. David asked him a couple of questions, but he did not spend a lot of time deliberating. Just as David did, we can and occasionally should ignore our detractors.

One of the best ways to kick the worry habit once and for all is never to invest our emotional well-being in the criticism of others. Often, ignoring an emotional charge is the best way to respond to it. We try to be logical and rational in our response, but arguments that are void of logic and rationality usually do not respond well to logic and rational thinking. It is very difficult to reason an emotional argument to a successful conclusion.

Here is a Marshall Proverb: "Convince a fool against his will, and he holds the same opinion still." When we attempt to reason with someone whose argument is not reasonable, our frustration level simply increases.

Suppose I'm trying to convince someone that a blue car is better than a white car. How do they argue against that? They don't. There is no logic to my argument, so it is senseless to try to fight it with logic. The best way is to ignore it. If we will do what David did and ignore those who want to argue with us with no rational foundation, we will be able to overcome many emotional obstacles and save ourselves a tremendous amount of turmoil. We have to be smart enough to know when we are in an emotional argument. Many of our arguments are only emotional. In our minds we have convinced ourselves that we have a valid argument, but it is emotional.

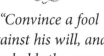

"Convince a fool against his will, and he holds the same opinion still."

If we try to deal with emotional obstacles by taking them on, this is what happens. We say, "Look what he did to me. He falsely accused me. I've got to get him back. I can't let him talk to me like that! I've got to stand up for my honor, integrity, and dignity." That, however, is not the way to battle an emotional argument. Too many people try to present a rational argument to confront an emotional obstacle. It just doesn't work.

Positional obstacles

Not only are there emotional obstacles, but there are also positional obstacles. Positional obstacles seek to control us. After David had the interaction with his brother Eliab, King Saul heard about David and sent for him. Look at the positional order. Saul was the king and had a position over David, so he sent for David. David's relationship with his brother was simply emotional—but his relationship with Saul was positional, because Saul, as king, was over him.

Now we not only have an emotional obstacle, but we also have a positional obstacle. Even King Saul criticized David, making an issue of his age. "Then Saul said to David, 'You are not able to go against this Philistine to fight with him; for you are but a youth while he has been a warrior from his youth'" (1 Samuel 17:33). Saul made an argument based on David's young age and lack of experience.

Notice what David did. David never got upset. There is nothing in the text that indicates that David was ever upset or angry. He kept his eyes and thoughts focused on what he had in mind; he knew that God was going to give him the victory. He was not sidetracked with what was being said and what was going on around him. He didn't allow the critiques and the obstacles to get him off course. When we decide to do battle with our giants, we must not let anything or anyone detour us.

Was Saul going to battle with the giant? Saul had been a great warrior. He was older, no doubt, than Goliath, so why didn't he go fight? Isn't that interesting? People will criticize us for not doing what they are afraid to do.

Why was Saul so critical? Let us look at Saul in a different way than we looked at Eliab. Saul was in a position of authority. So perhaps he felt some responsibility for David. Maybe he thought that if he allowed David to go out and fight and he got hurt, he would be responsible for allowing a person who is young and inexperienced to be in harm's way.

That is a positional obstacle. We, too, will face positional obstacles. We can worry about them, or we can do something about them. How do we overcome them? Sometimes we are in a relationship with people who are legitimately over us. What do we do when we see something that they do not? How did David deal with the critique of Saul? Notice the difference. When it was Eliab, it was an emotional situation, so David ignored him. With Saul, however, it was a positional situation, so David informed him. In essence, he said, "Saul, I know that you are the king and that you are in authority over me, but there is something you don't understand—something that you have not considered."

> But David said to Saul, "Your servant was tending his father's sheep. When a lion or a bear came and took a lamb from the flock, I went out after him and attacked him, and rescued it from his mouth; and when he rose up against me, I seized him by his beard and struck him and killed him. Your servant has killed both the lion and the bear; and this uncircumcised Philistine will be like one of them, since he has taunted the armies of the living God." And David said, "The Lord who delivered me from the paw of the lion and from the paw of the bear, He will deliver me from the hand of this Philistine." And Saul said to David, "Go, and may the Lord be with you" (1 Samuel 16:34-37).

Saul presented a rational argument. He was concerned about David's welfare, but when David informed him of what Saul did not know, Saul said, "Go right ahead." Sometimes we think that people in authority—those who are over us—are making an emotional argument, but there may be some rationale to their argument. If we dismiss a rational argument and claim that it is just emotional, we miss an opportunity to inform them.

Children usually think that their parents are trying to teach them only on an emotional level. I tell children that if they have a rational argument, ask the parents, "May I offer another opinion or perspective?" Hopefully, the parents will allow them to share their information. Why? Because they might not be making an emotional argument. If the child thinks the argument is emotional and thinks his parents are not going to listen, he could be ignoring what is actually a rational argument, and if that is the case, he really ought to be respectfully informing them.

David knew that Saul was making a positional argument, so he informed him. Positional obstacles are usually rational or have some rational foundation. That is why we can counter them with rationality. If an argument is rational, usually we can reason it to a successful conclusion. There are many obstacles on the battlefield, but there may be many more on the way to the battlefield. That is why I say that winning the war might be easier than getting to the battle. If, however, we know the enemies we face—emotional obstacles and positional obstacles—and know we must overcome them and how we can do so, we will be successful. The reason is not because we are clever, but because God wants us to be successful. He wants us to get over the hurdles on our way to the battle. Whether they are emotional or positional, He wants us to allow nothing to keep us from doing battle with the giants that are in our lives. He wants to help us. He wants to give us His Holy Spirit. He wants to provide a family fellowship for us. Through His Son, Jesus, He makes us holy and righteous. Our position gives us courage and confidence in the wisdom of God to battle the little giants that confront us. In doing so, we will be just like David—successful on the battlefield, and successful on the way to the battlefield.

Put your faith into action and stop worrying.

After the death of Moses, Joshua and the Israelites camped on the east bank of the Jordan River. Usually, the spring flood turned the Jordan into a turbulent torrent, yet on the other side rose the Land of Promise, which God had promised to the Israelites simply for the taking.

Who in their right mind would dare venture through this torrent without the promise of God? Even Joshua, with all his military might, dared not go forward without the promise from God of an ultimate victory. Because he knew of God's promise, he made his most difficult first move. Joshua could have stood on the west side wringing his hands in worry. He could have wasted precious time worrying about the unknown, but he did not. He sent spies to gather the facts:

> Then Joshua the son of Nun sent two men as spies secretly from Shittim, saying, "Go, view the land, especially Jericho." So they went and came into the house of a harlot whose name was Rahab, and lodged there... Then the two men returned and came down from the hill country and crossed over and came to Joshua the son of Nun, and they related to him all that had

happened to them. They said to Joshua, "Surely the Lord has given all the land into our hands; moreover, all the inhabitants of the land have melted away before us" (Joshua 2:1, 23-24).

Their report provided concrete information and thus eliminated the need for speculative imagination. Now the leader of Israel knew first hand both the promise of God and the situation in the Promised Land. We would do well to study and copy Joshua's two-pronged approach to battle: (1) know the promise of God and (2) know the situation in the Promised Land. God only knows how many worries this two-pronged approach would eliminate.

God promised to Israel the Land of Canaan, and they were to inhabit it "by any means necessary." Yet, they needed to know about the giants in the land. Knowing what they would encounter and believing that God would enable them should have strengthened their faith. Unfortunately for them and too often for us, knowing the gravity of the situation destroyed their confidence in the promise of God. Why does God need to win another battle to convince us that He can win battles? Hasn't He won enough to cause us to believe from now through eternity?

Slay the giant that worries us.

What are some of the giants that we battle? What are some of the giants that worry us? What are some of the giants that surface every day, the ones we worry about even while we're sleeping, the ones we plan to attack in a magnificent battle, but run in the opposite direction as soon as we face them?

Why does God need to win another battle to convince us that He can win battles?

Is it the backyard bully who makes life miserable for us? The one who taunts us every time we go in or out of the house? Is it the situation in our work place where we've been treated unfairly, but about which we dread talking to our superiors or confronting the guilty party? It could be the situation that causes us to lie awake all night saying, "They mistreated me. They knowingly mistreated me, and I need to say something about it," but for whatever reason, we do not. Is it the credit-card debt? Our wayward child? The roof over our head that gets smaller and more leaky by the month?

Each of us has faced a giant that taunted us and still causes us worry. There are circumstances, issues, and people that we need to confront. It may come as a surprise to learn that God wants us to do battle with our giants. In fact, He even challenges us to do battle with the chief giant: "Submit therefore to God. Resist the devil and he will flee from you" (James 4:7). And He gives us a battle plan not only to fight, but to be encouraged in the fight:

> Be of sober spirit, be on the alert. Your adversary, the devil, prowls around like a roaring lion, seeking someone to devour. But resist him, firm in your faith, knowing that the same experiences of suffering are being accomplished by your brethren who are in the world (1 Peter 5:8-9).

In other words, God sanctions our address of those things that have taunted us. He says the time has come that those things will no longer have an impact on our lives—those things that for too many years have manipulated us into looking and behaving like weaklings. God wants us to confront, and He knows that once we do, they will no longer worry us. Remember, when we are worried, the people and situations that worry us are in control; when we, in partnership with God Himself, are concerned rather than worried and take action to eliminate the problems, we allow God to be in control.

We will stop worrying and take action when three things happen. First, we will stop worrying and take action when our positive courage outweighs our negative fears. Often times, the fear of taking control and doing battle is enough to keep us in the very bondage that worries us. When our positive courage outweighs our negative fears, however, we will at long last do battle with the giants. Those who do battle with their giants may still be somewhat fearful, but at some point their positive courage has exceeded their fears, and they go to war.

Under ordinary circumstances, a ninety-five pound mother will not do battle with a 350-pound man. When the safety of her child is threatened, however, she will not only go to battle, but will win the war. What happened? She forgot about how small she was and how large he was; in other words, her positive courage outweighed her negative fear. When our positive courage outweighs our negative fear, we, too, will go to battle, and be successful.

Second, we will stop worrying and take action when we have a passion for God to get His glory. In fact, our positive courage increases according to our passion for God to get His glory. When there is a burning passion within us and there is an overwhelming desire for God to get His glory, our positive courage rises. David recognized that Israel was embarrassed by the taunts of Goliath, the uncircumcised Philistine. Circumcision was a sign of the covenant, and those of the covenant enjoyed the favor of God. In this instance, however, those with the favor of God were afraid of those without the favor of God. This is the exact opposite of the way it should have been. God was not getting the glory due His name.

No doubt, David shook his head in amazement and said, "How in the world is this happening?" How astonishing to find an uncircumcised Philistine taunting the armies of the living God—and getting away with it. David knew that something was wrong. God was not getting His glory. Therefore, David asked, "Who is this man?" There was a burning passion within David for God to get His glory, and that is where David centered his strategy. He had access to all the finest weapons of the army of Israel, yet he chose to use the most low-tech piece of gear available—a slingshot and five smooth stones. Humans had designed the other battle weapons, but David chose not to rely on anything for which humans could claim the credit.

> "Your servant has killed both the lion and the bear; and this uncircumcised Philistine will be like one of them, since he has taunted the armies of the living God"...Then David said to the Philistine, "You come to me with a sword, a spear, and a javelin, but I come to you in the name of the Lord of hosts, the God of the armies of Israel, whom you have taunted. This day the Lord will deliver you up into my hands, and I will strike you down

and remove your head from you. And I will give the dead bodies of the army of the Philistines this day to the birds of the sky and the wild beasts of the earth, that all the earth may know that there is a God in Israel" (1 Samuel 17:36, 45-46).

God had lost His glory because the army's behavior caused those who observed to ask, "Where is the God of Israel? We heard about the God who brought the people out of the land of Egypt and opened the Red Sea. We heard about the God who did all these things, but where is He now?" David pondered on those things, and we can imagine the passion rise within him saying, "I have a desire for God to get His glory!" When there is a passion within us for God to get His glory, our positive courage begins to increase. The key is that we must consider the cause. This battle with Goliath was not about David; it was about God getting His glory.

Third, we will stop worrying and take action when we have a pleasure to get our gift. No wonder David asked, "What will be done for the man who kills this Philistine?" He learned that the man who killed the Philistine would be handsomely rewarded.

In the late 1970's, while living in Memphis, Tennessee, I visited the office of a young man named, perhaps not by coincidence, David. He was an entrepreneurial opportunist. David's neighbor had encountered a severe problem; sewage had flooded his basement. The neighbor asked David if he knew someone who could fix the problem. David began pondering who would tackle such a task. As he thought, the neighbor said, "I have already gone to the credit union and got the money."

David said, "You have what?" The neighbor repeated that he already had the money to repair the problem, and just needed someone to do it. Not being one to let an opportunity to make a few dollars slip past, David spoke up and said, "I will repair it for you."

When David's desire to get his gift overrode his fear of tackling the basement problem, he consented to do battle with the sewer pipes. The fact that the man already had the money caught his attention. There was something in it for him.

Likewise, it was a pleasure for the shepherd-boy David to get the gift promised to the person who slew the giant. The promise was that the king himself would shower the victor with funds, and even give him the privilege of marrying the king's own daughter. What could be better than becoming the rich son-in-law to the king? In addition, his father's house and descendants would live tax free in Israel without having to render public service or go to war.

David heard all this and quickly tuned into the station WIIFM (what's in it for me). He considered the cause and counted the cost. It really didn't cost him, of course; it paid. When it becomes a pleasure for us to get our gift, we will go after it. When we perceive that God gets things done because we work and cooperate with Him, He works and cooperates with us.

Because David believed that God should get His glory, David saw no reason to be afraid of Goliath, and he wanted others to stop being afraid, too (see verse 32). Because David wanted his gift, he was willing to do battle with Goliath.

King Saul still was unconvinced of David's ability to battle Goliath (see verse 33). To illustrate further the basis of his confidence, David was ready with his resume, and told how he had rescued lambs from the mouths of lions and bears (see verses 34-37). After that rescue effort, he killed the attacking animals. He believed that just as God would want him to protect his sheep, God would also want someone to protect His sheep, Israel. Certainly, if he had the favor of God to retrieve a lamb from its enemy, surely he would have the favor of God to retrieve Israel from its enemies.

This is the "greater than, less than" theology that Jesus emphasized during His earthly ministry. If God takes care of the ravens, who are of less value to God than human beings, then certainly He will take care of human beings, who are of greater value to Him than the ravens (see Luke 12:24). Our history should be a courage instiller and motivation booster for us when we face battles. Indeed, we should realize our positional value with God and trust His promises.

David attributed to God the glory of his success rescuing the lamb. He was therefore willing to give God the glory for the victory of succeeding in battle with Goliath. David recognized three things: (1) Something had to be done to Goliath in order for God to get His glory; (2) something had to be done to Goliath in order for David to get His gift, and (3) something would never happen unless God worked through him. It was the partnership of a human and the Divine working together that was critical for Goliath to be destroyed.

This may be a paradigm shift for many believers. When we think that God alone will do it by Himself, we become long-term prayer warriors. Prayer alone just activates and promotes the elements that bring about change. Prayer alone does not always get the job done. To succeed, prayer requires a faith application.

No doubt, the armies of Israel had been praying for forty days: "God, deliver us from this giant! Lord, do something with him. Give him a quick case of AIDS or something. Lord, please deliver us!" No doubt, they were praying for that, but they were doing little else. If we think that God is going to do it all, we become timid and lazy. We just pray and wait. There are Christians who say, "I just keep praying. I'm waiting on God. I've been praying for nine months. I've been praying for sixteen years."

God is waiting for us to do something. Israel could have prayed the rest of their lives and Goliath would have still been coming out every morning saying, "Come on over and let's do battle." When we think that God is going to do it by Himself, that is what happens. Conversely when we think that we are going to do it by ourselves, we become arrogant. David was not arrogant. He recognized that he must do something and that God was going to work with him and through him. God would insure His victory.

God wants us to do battle with the giants that intimidate us and keep us from doing His work. The work of God takes place outside the walls of worship. Too often we become just like the armies of Israel. We dress for the occasion. We come together in our holy huddle and discuss the work. In unison, we say, "Amen!" We go out of the building, see the wicked of the world, the deterioration of the family, the proliferation of drugs, the rising unemployment parading in front of our door daring us to come and do battle. We go back into our holy huddle and pray some more. Will the real David please stand up?

We've been doing that for years just like the armies of Israel. We are fearful and afraid to do battle with the things that cause us not to actively engage in changing our world for good. We need to begin changing one heart at a time. We must sit down and talk to people about our relationship with God—our relationship with God through Christ that translates into a more productive "everyday" person. We must show them how they can come to enjoy what we enjoy.

Why did David visit his brothers? He did so to provide nourishment for them. Why did his father send nourishment? He did so because he thought that his sons, along with the army of Israel, were engaged in fighting the Philistines (see verse 19). Were they fighting? Jesse thought he was sending food to the fighting soldiers—but we know they were standing on the bank of the river scared to death. As a matter of fact, they were not even in the valley. They had not gone down to the battlefield.

Often we are consuming our resources, even asking for additional assistance, while we remain in our holy huddle discussing the battle. What a waste of resources. Oh, we talk a good game and to some it seems like we are going to do something. God wants us to do battle with the giants that cause us not to get involved actively in reaching the lost. When will that happen? When we possess a passion for God to get His glory, we will stop worrying about the giants and go to war against the giants.

People with no direction live raggedy lives. When God's people begin to point to Him as the way, we can change things. Instead, God loses His glory and is embarrassed in the eyes of those who are around us. Non-believers have the right to ask, "What value is the believer?" Really, what impact are we making in the lives of those with whom we interact? Can they adequately and accurately say that as a result of our influence nothing has gotten better? If that is the case, then God doesn't get His glory. When there is a burning passion within us for God to get His glory, we will open the Bible and we will talk to folk about the good news of salvation that is in Christ Jesus. When there is a passion within us for God to get His glory, when it is a passion within us to see lives changed—for people to be snatched back from the brink of disaster, for drug addicts to get their lives together, for folk who are contemplating divorce to reconcile, for children who have been disobedient to their parents to began to live consistently with their parents' wishes—I'm telling you that God will get His glory.

We will always balk at executing the great commission (see Matthew 28:19) until we come to grips with the great commandment (see Matthew 22:36-40). The great commission is, "Go into all the world and make disciples and teach them to observe all that God commands." The great commandment is, "Love with all your heart." When we have obeyed the great commandment, we will then obey the great commission.

The rest of 1 Samuel chapter 17 tells how David prevailed over Goliath.

> Thus David prevailed over the Philistine with a sling and a stone, and he struck the Philistine and killed him; but there was no sword in David's hand. Then David ran and stood over the Philistine and took his sword and drew it out of its sheath and killed him, and cut off his head with it. When the Philistines saw that their champion was dead, they fled (1 Samuel 17:50-51).

There are other giant "wannabees." They are looking at that giant and they too are taunting us. Once we do battle with the giant, however, the giant "wannabees" flee. Notice what the remainder of the Philistine army did when Goliath fell: "The men of Israel and Judah arose and shouted and pursued the Philistines as far as the valley" (verse 52). When we do battle with the giant, not only does that destroy the other wannabee giants, but it also increases courage in the folk on our side.

If you have read this far in the book and realize that you have been afraid to do battle with the giants that have caused you worry for years, are you ready to make a change? Or do you want to continue being controlled by and overwhelmed by worry? This is a critical time for you, a time of decision. Are you ready to make a change, in spite of your fears, or do you want to live the way you always have, consumed by worry? It is time to do battle so that God can get His glory. Remember, you do not fight alone. Like David, you are battling alongside the lion of Judah, the one who is victorious, and who promises you victory, also. God does not get any glory when you continue to be defeated and afraid. It is time for you to be victorious, and for Him to get the glory in all areas of your life.

Thought Provokers

1 What worries have controlled you to the point that you have been afraid to face the giants in your life?

2 What obstacles have kept you from the battlefield?

3 What are you going to do about it?

Chapter 7

YOUR PRACTICAL PROGRAM FOR OVERCOMING WORRY

BELIEVE THAT AN ARTICULATE understanding of the promises of God should reduce or eliminate worrying. That is the foundation of this book. If, however, I have not fully convinced you by my understanding of the principles of Scripture, then I have no other recourse but to leave you to your own interpretation of the word of God. Therefore, I insist that you write in this book your understanding of God as you read His words.

"In peace I will both lie down and sleep, for You alone, O Lord, make me to dwell in safety" (Psalm 4:8).

_____

_____

_____

"He who dwells in the shelter of the Most High will abide in the shadow of the Almighty. I will say to the Lord, 'My refuge and my fortress, My God, in whom I trust!'" (Psalm 91:1-2).

_____

_____

_____

"Those who love Your law have great peace, and nothing causes them to stumble" (Psalm 119:165).

_____

_____

_____

"When you lie down, you will not be afraid; when you lie down, your sleep will be sweet" (Proverbs 3:24).

_____

_____

_____

"The steadfast of mind You will keep in perfect peace, because he trusts in You" (Isaiah 26:3).

_____

_____

_____

"Do not let your heart be troubled; believe in God, believe also in Me" (John 14:1).

_____

_____

_____

"Peace I leave with you; My peace I give to you; not as the world gives do I give to you. Do not let your heart be troubled, nor let it be fearful" (John 14:27).

_____

_____

_____

"For the mind set on the flesh is death, but the mind set on the Spirit is life and peace" (Romans 8:6).

_____

_____

_____

"Be anxious for nothing, but in everything by prayer and supplication with thanksgiving let your requests be made known to God. And the peace of God, which surpasses all comprehension, will guard your hearts and your minds in Christ Jesus" (Philippians 4:6-7).

_____

_____

_____

"And my God will supply all your needs according to His riches in glory in Christ Jesus" (Philippians 4:19).

_____

_____

_____

"Let the peace of Christ rule in your hearts, to which indeed you were called in one body; and be thankful" (Colossians 3:15).

_____

_____

_____

"Therefore humble yourselves under the mighty hand of God, that He may exalt you at the proper time, casting all your anxiety on Him, because He cares for you" (1 Peter 5:6-7).

_____

_____

_____

FOR THE RECORD

Within Scripture, a distinct organism called the church existed. *Before* the death, burial, and resurrection, of Jesus Christ, Scripture declared that the church *would* come into existence (see Matthew 16:17-18). *After* the death, burial, and resurrection of Jesus Christ, Scripture declared that the church had *already* come into existence (see Acts 8:1-3).

The preaching of the death, burial, and resurrection of Jesus Christ resulted in people becoming forgiven of sins (see Acts 2:36-38). The preaching of the death, burial, and resurrection of Jesus Christ resulted in people becoming saved (see Acts 2:47). The preaching of the death, burial, and resurrection of Jesus Christ resulted in people becoming members of the church (see Acts 2:47).

Becoming forgiven of sins is equivalent to becoming saved, which is equivalent to becoming a member of the church. Those who are forgiven have become saved. Those who are saved are members of the church. One cannot become a member of the church without becoming saved. One cannot become saved without becoming a member of the church. So, to be saved is to be in the church, and to be in the church is the same as being saved.

The church, the body of Christ, came to exist only after the resurrection of Jesus. Christianity rises and/or falls on the resurrection of Jesus. The resurrection is more than a contemporary Easter idea; it is the very essence of Christianity. Christians pledge themselves not to a festive holiday program, but to a person, the resurrected Lord Jesus Christ.

The message of the death, burial, and resurrection of Jesus brought the church into existence. An appropriate response of faith toward the death, burial, and resurrection of Jesus brings a person into a forgiven state, saved, and into the church.

Believing that Jesus is the Christ, the Son of God, is an adequate response of faith. The death, burial, and resurrection of Jesus proves that He is the Christ, the Son of God (see Romans 1:1-4, Acts 17:30-31). Therefore, only those who believe can become forgiven of sins, saved, and members of the church (see John 8:24, Acts 4:1-4, 8:35-37).

Repenting of sin is an adequate response of faith. Repentance is the change of heart within a person (see Matthew 21:28-32). In repentance, you change your allegiance (see Acts 2:38, 17:30, 26:19-20). You remove your allegiance to your selfish self and pledge your allegiance to the Savior.

Becoming baptized is an adequate response of faith. Baptism is your response to the call of God (see 1 Peter 3:21). Near the beginning of his ministry, the apostle Peter preached about baptism. Near the end of his ministry, the apostle

Peter wrote about baptism. Even now baptism saves. What is baptism?

First, we consider the dry side of baptism. It is a response of the mind, for it is an internal appeal toward God. The dry side is a response of the conscience. The conscience is a product of accepted teachings (see John 8:1-9, Leviticus 20:10). The dry side is a response of a *good* conscience. Within this context, a good conscience is a heart that trusts in the resurrection of Jesus Christ (see 1 Peter 3:21). The resurrection proves that Jesus is the son of God (see Romans 1:4, Acts 17:31). Only those who believe in the resurrection of Jesus have a good conscience for baptism (see John 8:24, Acts 8:35-37). If your conscience is insufficiently taught, your conscience will be insufficiently developed. And if your conscience is incorrectly taught, then it will be incorrectly developed.

Baptism takes place while the penitent believer is in water (see Acts 8:36-39). Baptism consists of taking the penitent believer to the water, and never bringing the water to the penitent believer. We should never attempt to reduce baptism to sprinkling and pouring of water. Some object to the necessity of being covered in water, but Jesus was sealed in His tomb (see Matthew 27:62-64, Romans 6:4). Some object to the necessity of water, yet water is specifically mentioned (see Acts 8:36-39, 10:47, 1 Peter 3:20-21). God refused to heal Naaman until he went into the water (see 2 Kings 5:14).

When those who heard the gospel believed, repented, and became baptized, they were forgiven, saved, and became a member of the church. Even now, a faith response to the death, burial, and resurrection of Jesus Christ allows one to become forgiven of sins, saved, and a Christian.

How much must one know before becoming baptized? I favor teaching an abundance of truth, yet we must ask, how much does the Scripture indicate that believers knew before they became baptized? How can we know how much a person knows? We know how much a person knows only by how much they indicate that they know. How much did early believers indicate they knew before being baptized? They indicated only that they believed that Jesus was the son of God (see Acts 8:37).

Believers need to know how to worship, where to worship, the nature of the church, and how to behave as a Christian, yet early believers were never called upon to demonstrate that level of knowledge prior to becoming baptized. Saying that one has become a Christian differs from saying that one has learned how to behave as a Christian (see Matthew 28:18-20). Some have become Christians, yet are worshipping in error. We must call them out of all religious error.

Who can baptize? The status of the one who teaches and baptizes has no effect upon the resulting state of the penitent believer. If it did, believers would be held responsible for what they could not possibly know, for no person can really know the heart of another.

Where must one be baptized? One can be baptized any place there is adequate water for a burial. Remember that only those who have believed, repented, and become baptized have become forgiven of sins, saved, and a member of the church. Nevertheless, all those who have believed, repented, and become baptized have become forgiven of sins, saved, and a member of the church.

Why is there so much confusion on subject of baptism? An intellectual exegesis of Scripture (bringing out of the text the ideas of the author) rather than an emotional exegesis of Scripture (bringing into the text the ideas of the reader) peels away most of the layers of confusion. The Holy Spirit could not come until after Jesus had risen from the dead and ascended to Heaven (see John 16:7). Some forty days after Jesus had risen from the dead, the Holy Spirit was yet to come (see Acts 1:1-8). The Holy Spirit came on the day of Pentecost (see Acts 2:1-4). The Holy Spirit revealed the message of truth to those who wrote Scripture (see Ephesians 3:1-5, 2 Peter 1:21). The apostle Peter spoke the words of Acts 2:38 before Matthew, Mark, Luke, and John wrote the words contained in their gospels. Being from regions beyond Jerusalem, most of those who heard the words of Acts 2:38 had not heard Jesus speak (see Acts 2:9-11). Even those who had heard Jesus speak failed to understand His message; therefore they crucified Him (see Acts 3:17, 1 Corinthians 2:8).

Historically, the Jews offered sacrifices with an understanding that they would invoke the forgiveness (appeasement) of God. Even on Pentecost, they believed that they needed to respond in order to receive forgiveness of God. Therefore, they asked, "What shall we do?" (see Acts 2:37). Peter had just preached a persuasive sermon designed to convince the audience that Jesus was the Christ and Lord (see Acts 2:36). Obviously, some who heard also believed, for their hearts were pricked (see Acts 2:37). Hearts are never pricked until belief comes. In addition to believing, they asked what to do. In other words, they were now asking, "After believing, what (else) shall we do?"

If they had been forgiven (saved) just by believing, Peter should have told them so. If they had been saved just by believing, Peter misled them by allowing them to believe that there was something they needed to do in order to be saved. In the past, they had killed and offered an animal in their effort to receive forgiveness of sins. Peter informed them that no longer would they have to kill a lamb. The lamb (Jesus) had already been slain. Now, they must repent and be baptized to embrace the death of Jesus. Only after Jesus had been raised from the dead did He make the connection or correlate baptism with salvation (see Mark 16:16). No wonder then that Peter relates baptism to salvation (see Acts 2:38).

But what about Romans 10:9-10? Let's set the stage.

1. Those to whom the apostle Paul addressed this letter were called and had become saints (see Romans 1:6-7).

2. They had died to sin (see Romans 6:2).

3. They had been baptized into Christ and His death (see Romans 6:3).

4. They had been raised from the dead to walk in the newness of life (see Romans 6:4).

5. They had become united with Jesus (see Romans 6:5).

6. Their old self had been crucified with Christ (see Romans 6:6).

7. They had obeyed from the heart the doctrinal teachings (see Romans 6:17).

8. They had been freed from sin (see Romans 6:18).

9. They had become servants of righteousness (see Romans 6:18).

10. Jews from Rome had been in Jerusalem on Pentecost (see Acts 2:10). It is likely they were baptized at that time.

Therefore, the apostle Paul said to the believers—those who had already been baptized—"Confess and believe" (see Romans 10:9-10).

What about Ephesians 2:8, which states, "For by grace you have been saved through faith"? The Ephesians had heard the message of truth (see Ephesians 1:13a). They had believed the message of truth (see Ephesians 1:13b). They had been baptized (see Acts 19:1-5). In Acts 8:30-32, the eunuch did not understand what he was reading from Isaiah chapter 53. Philip began at Isaiah 53:7, the place where the eunuch was reading, and preached Jesus to him (see Acts 8:35).

1. How could Philip preach Jesus when the name Jesus is not once stated in Isaiah chapter 53?

2. How could Philip demand that the eunuch believe that Jesus Christ is the Son of God when believing that Jesus Christ is the Son of God is never stated in Isaiah chapter 53?

3. How could Philip introduce the subject of baptism while preaching Jesus from Isaiah chapter 53 when baptism is not stated in Isaiah chapter 53?

4. How did Philip understand Isaiah chapter 53 when the eunuch did not?

The answers to all four questions are the same. Philip had a Holy Spirit-led post-resurrection understanding of the Old Testament (see Acts 6:5) and the eunuch did not. God more fully revealed His will to the apostles and prophets (see Ephesians 3:5). Philip had heard the message from the apostles in Jerusalem (see Acts 6:1-5). There are some things that had not been understood before, but came to be understood only after the resurrection of Jesus.

Because Philip had a Holy Spirit-led post-resurrection understanding of the Old Testament, God enlightened him to understand things more fully than others understood. God enlightened His apostles and prophets to understand the Old Testament. When we read the New Testament, we gain insight into the inspired minds of the apostles and prophets (see Ephesians 3:5). Jesus recognized that men needed a post-resurrection understanding of the Old Testament scriptures. Therefore, He opened their minds to understand them (see Luke 24:44-47). God opened Lydia's mind to understand (see Acts 16:14); her understanding led her to be baptized (see Acts 16:15). The Corinthians had been baptized (see Acts 18:8). Earlier, Paul alluded to their baptism (see 1 Corinthians 6:8-11). He even reminded them of the role of baptism in the deliverance of the Israelites (see 1 Corinthians 10:1-4).

Where does the Old Testament teach the purpose of baptism? It does not. It just illustrates it. The lamb's blood became available for the Israelites (see Exodus 12:21-28), yet the Israelites were not free from bondage until they passed through the sea (see Exodus 14:26-29). God saved Israel on the day that they passed through the water (see Exodus 14:30). The Holy Spirit's inspired commentary called that experience a baptism:

> For I do not want you to be unaware, brethren, that our fathers were all under the cloud, and all passed through the sea; and all were baptized into Moses in the cloud and in the sea; and all ate the same spiritual food; and all drank the same spiritual drink, for they were drinking from a spiritual rock which followed them; and the rock was Christ (1 Corinthians 10:1-4).

Scripture does provide a roadmap toward the salvation that is found only in Christ Jesus. We can ascertain the will of God through reading Scripture. Obedience to this guidance results in the best possible life on earth as well as positions us for the best possible life beyond this earth.

FOR MORE INFORMATION

For further information about John Marshall, his ministry, and his ministry resources, please contact him at:

John Marshall Enterprises
PO Box ~~878~~ 2136
~~Pine Lake,~~ Georgia 30072
Stone Mountain (404) 316-5525
www.graceview.us
jdm@graceview.us

OTHER BOOKS BY JOHN MARSHALL

Good and Angry: A Personal Guide to Anger Management

God, Listen! Prayers That God Always Answers (includes addiction-recovery guide)

The Power of the Tongue: What You Say Is What You Get

Final Answer: You Asked, God Answered

Success Is a God Idea

Show Me the Money: 7 Exercises That Build Economic Strength

CPSIA information can be obtained at www.ICGtesting.com
Printed in the USA
LVOW05s0511300914

406508LV00001B/5/A